A CHRISTIANITY THAT REALLY WORKS

RON MARR

 Whitaker House

Unless otherwise indicated, all Scripture quotations are taken from the *New King James Version* (NKJV), © 1979, 1980, 1982 by Thomas Nelson, Inc. Used by permission. All rights reserved.

All Scripture quotations marked (KJV) are from the *King James Version* of the Holy Bible.

A CHRISTIANITY THAT REALLY WORKS

ISBN: 0-88368-271-0
Printed in the United States of America
© 1993 by ChristLife, Inc.

Whitaker House
30 Hunt Valley Circle
New Kensington, PA 15068

6 7 8 9 10 11 12 / 08 07 06 05 04 03 02 01

Introduction

How I praise God for introducing me to a Christianity that really works—and for the privilege of sharing it with you. I am unworthy of the task. My heart still aches that over the years I have grieved my Lord so terribly and hurt so many folks. I repent and revel in His marvelous love, mercy, and grace, and beg the forgiveness of all I have injured.

I have found most of the Lord's people are similarly disappointed with their Christian lives, and I want to offer them the help with which the Lord has helped me. Most believe that Christianity really does work—or at least it's supposed to. But for many, it doesn't quite seem to—not as they would like, anyway.

This book is written especially for you who are the lonely, the hurting, the discouraged, the suffering, the anxious, and the fearful. It is for those who want to walk more closely with their God in the intimacy of a shared love that goes beyond the passing nature of mere feelings. It is written for all God's children who want a Christianity that really works.

This book offers no simplistic solutions. It encourages all of us to cast ourselves upon our heavenly Father and find in Him the *"peace which surpasses all understanding,"* (Philippians 4:7) and all else our hearts really need.

Out of the Cauldron

Every thought here reflects something of my personal preparation in learning to walk with the Lord. Still, I've tried to avoid urging any of my personal experiences on my readers as though they were normative for all. It would not make much sense for me to make any of my experiences a standard for anyone else.

How could I? Every time I have thought I'd arrived, the experience disappeared like a puff of smoke. Every time I thought I'd reached a new plateau of obedience, it would be only to see more of my sin and failure. How I thank God it's been so. How else could He keep me from substituting some incident, some feeling, or some supposed achievement for Himself to my eternal loss?

He alone is my life, my hope, my joy, my peace, my righteousness, my wisdom, my sanctification, my redemption, my all. There is no real enduring happiness or contentment apart from Him. Only as I rest contentedly at home in Him as He is in me is my relationship with Him full of reality and unending hope.

Uniquely Yours

He is your all, too, if He is your Savior. And such you must find Him—but not my way, not anyone else's way, rather His way for you.

You are unique, and He will be uniquely yours. Don't try to mimic anyone else. Let the Holy Spirit alone be your teacher and guide.

How to Read This Book

If you're impatient to get to the meat of the message, read the addendum. If you want answers to practical concerns, turn to the chapters of practical hints and summary outlines. But best of all, start at the beginning and patiently read through in humble reliance on the Lord.

To get maximum benefit, take this book in bite-sized chunks that can be easily chewed and digested. Soak its reading in confident prayer that He'll reveal Himself to you and draw you close to Himself. Underline it. Meditate on it. Note your questions, concerns, and comments in its margins. Carry it with you. When you've laid it down, return to it again and again.

Take it into your times alone with the Lord. Keep it and your Bible open in front of you. Look up Scriptures cited but not quoted.

Only God Can Draw You to Himself

Depend on the Holy Spirit to enlighten you and enable you to begin practicing what you read as He sets His seal of approval on it. Please don't think for a moment, because I've suggested approaches to the development of your relationship with the Lord that you or I can initiate anything good; instead, let Him teach you to be quietly content that He is in you and you are in Him. Watch Him work in you to will and to do of His good pleasure.

My only really significant purpose is to point you to the Lord Himself as the answer to every longing of your heart. How well I point you to Him will determine this book's real worth. I hope I've kept it easy to read and understand so it can bless, encourage, and challenge all God's children. May the Holy Spirit use these words to help you learn to live in continuous personal revival as you dwell in the Father's love.

Contents

Introduction

1. The Wonder of It All 9
2. Oh, To Be Needy 19
3. Oh, To Be Dependent 27
4. None But the Humble Heart 37
5. None But the Hungry Heart 45
6. God Is All We Need 51
7. The Way into the Heart of God 59
8. Communication & Communion 73
9. Practical Prayer Hints 83
10. The Prayer of Love 95
11. Dimensions of True Prayer 109
12. Overcoming Hindrances to Prayer . . . 117
13. The Emptying 129
14. The Golden Secret 137
15. Peace and Patience! 147
16. The Golden Key 157
17. Day by Day 165
18. Dynamic Life Out of Death 174
19. Applying the Cross 182
20. Walking in Liberty 192
21. Just Being Receptive 200
22. Come to Jesus 212
23. Looking to Jesus 218
24. God Really Can Be Trusted 224
25. The Subject of Failure 236
26. At Home in God 249
27. God Wants You to Be Happy 259

28. Back to Basics 271
29. Warning Flags 287
30. A System of Checks & Balances 297
31. Final Thoughts on Christ at Work . . 307
    Addendum 317

Christ in you, the hope of glory.
—Colossians 1:27

Of Him and through Him and to Him are all
things, to whom be glory forever. Amen.
—Romans 11:36

And you are complete in Him, who is the head
of all principality and power.
—Colossians 2:10

He that spared not His own Son,
but delivered Him up for us all,
how shall He not with Him
also freely give us all things?
—Romans 8:32

The humble He teaches His way.
—Psalm 25:9

Being confident of this very thing,
that He who has begun a good work in you
will complete it until the day of Jesus Christ.
—Philippians 1:6

CHAPTER 1

The Wonder of It All

*But now in Christ Jesus
you who once were far off have been brought
near by the blood of Christ.*
—*Ephesians 2:13*

It's shocking! It's wonderful! Your hope to get close to the heart of God is that you are a sinner and a failure!

A Christianity That Works?

The phone rang. The voice at the other end was anxiously strained. She had seen my article in *The Christian World Report* titled, *Do You Want a Christianity That Really Works?*

My caller **really** wanted her Christianity to work. She wanted it so desperately her heart was breaking. She felt she was worse off than she had been when she first accepted Christ. He'd delivered her from drugs and other evils, but she found herself still in bondage to smoking and a temper that had led her to swearing at her children again. Her guilt overwhelmed her. She felt hopeless and devastated when she heard such things from preachers as, "If you're carnal, you're not going to heaven."

I told her that her very failure, guilt, and hopelessness best qualified her to receive God's grace. I told her to cast herself on the Lord alone. I asked her to see Him not as Judge, but as her loving heavenly Father waiting to receive her with open arms of love. I encouraged her to let go of everything and rest in Him.

Later, I told my wife, "I could almost cry for the pain of that dear lady." But how glad I was that I was able to hold out hope to her. With the greatest delight, I offer that same hope to you.

The Curse of Works

My heart aches for the millions of the Lord's people who are being told to just straighten up and fly right. The church's great error today is the same works-righteousness that Paul was forced to expose and oppose in the earliest days of the Christian church. It's an awful legalistic thing, visiting on us nothing but perpetual failure and hopelessness.

The purpose of the law is to show us our total inability to please God and to serve as a *"schoolmaster to bring us unto Christ"* (Galatians 3:24 KJV). The law is a terribly hard master, whipping us with our failure to meet its demands, visiting on us condemnation and guilt. It shows us our impossibly hopeless sinfulness and neediness. For this we can be grateful—if we also see the hope there is for us in the free grace and mercy of God in Christ.

We're saved by God's grace alone. The wonder of God's grace is that our very sin and sinfulness, our very failure to please Him, qualify us for His mercy and full salvation.

Now, we accept this as true of our initial experience. We came in utter hopelessness to the Lord. He freely saved us from eternal death and hell and gave us the free gift of present salvation, eternal life, and heaven.

Always by Grace Alone

But are we content that we are qualified to receive God's grace and every other good gift He has for us always and only by our failure alone? Are we content to be nothing more than needy sinners dependent only on God and His grace? Or do we hope somehow to escape the stigma of sin and become "good" people?

Secretly, do you hope someday to find yourself somehow pleasing God and to some extent at least deserving His love by your good living? I honestly believe that virtually all of us do. We've relegated such thoughts as, *"There is none righteous, no, not one"* (Romans 3:10) to significance for the unsaved only.

A close Christian friend said in quick response to an obvious assumption on my part, "I'm not a sinner!" She really is a good person by human standards, and she likes to be a good person. Inadvertently, however, she had laid bare her self-righteousness.

God Hates Self-righteousness

That's what this hope in yourself actually is—self-righteousness. Do you know that there's nothing God hates more than self-righteousness? Do you really know what He thinks of self-righteousness? You should. You've probably heard Isaiah 64:6 often enough: *"All our righteousnesses are like filthy rags."* Dirty rags are not just unattractive: they breed disease, destruction, and death.

God Himself is the righteousness of His children. Only His righteousness in us ever will be anything other than filthy rags. If we think anything else, we're doomed to a lifetime of disappointment, frustration, and failure.

Not Good Enough

She lay on her deathbed as I visited her. In her voice was an unexpected hollowness caused not by her physical condition but by a haunting

12

fear coming from deep within. She'd been a Christian for many years, a Sunday School teacher, a godly mother, and a good witness for the Lord. But now she was expressing a fear that she wasn't altogether ready to face her Maker.

My surprise subsided as I realized it was this cursed self-righteousness revealing itself. She had seen herself as essentially a good person. Often she'd said, "I wouldn't do *that*."

Here it was on her deathbed haunting her. Oh, she knew all right that only Jesus and faith in His shed blood and finished work could get her into heaven. But what about her sin and failure? How could she face her Savior? She didn't deserve Him or His heaven!

How confused we are! That's exactly why we need His mercy and grace: *we don't deserve Him or His heaven.* Jesus alone is enough for us at heaven's gate. Only He! It's our failure, our incapacity in ourselves to please Him, that qualifies us for Him then, now, and during all the time intervening.

But Are We Looking for Him?

The problem is that we may not be looking for Him, but for something less, even for a Christianity that works. If we expect ever to be spiritually successful—to be good—we're in trouble.

13

We must expect only to be bad, always needy sinners with but one hope: Him. Finding Him sufficient, we must cast ourselves repeatedly on Him and His grace. We must lay ourselves down again and again in Him and rest in the assurance that Christ in us is our hope of glory, that we in Him are complete. He is the Christianity that works.

David was a man after God's own heart, but this wasn't because he was faultless. He was an adulterer and a murderer, sins he committed long years after he came to know and love the Lord! He was a man after God's own heart only because he was willing to be a sinner needing to turn to God again and again. He looked to his God in spite of his sin.

We come, not in our goodness, our righteousness, our holiness, but in Him and in His. We come counting on Him, His righteousness, and His undeserved mercy and grace. We look away from all else to Him. We lay ourselves down in His arms of love and rest there, where we receive Him as enough for right now—enough hope and help, enough mercy and grace, enough forgiveness, love, joy, peace, and all else we need.

This is the wonder of it all. Our sin and failure, our pain and hurt, our frustration with ourselves and our circumstances seem insurmountable. But His grace covers them all.

Be Real

You shall know the truth,
and the truth shall make you free.
—John 8:32

What is truth? Reality. What actually is.

This is part of what God meant when He said His name is I AM. He is real. There's nothing in Him that's unreal.

My dear one in Christ, be real. Be honest. Be the needy sinner you are. Face the truth about yourself, your sin, your failure, your need. If you feel that the idea of His being all you really need is too abstract for you, just be real enough to admit it. Trust Him to change your comprehension of that reality.

There's no happiness in playing the game of pretense in which we try to justify or excuse ourselves, or look to ourselves as our hope, when all the time we know better. Simply acknowledge that God is right in His condemnation of your actions, attitudes, and heart. Admit your need and inability. This opens the door to confession and repentance of all that displeases Him—and to real happiness!

But look out! We tend to see even confession and repentance as somehow earning God's acceptance or forgiveness. Never! His acceptance is ours through Christ alone, unmerited by us in any way. Our part is to live our entire lives in the continual realization that we are undeserving sinners and in constant appreciation for the gift of His mercy and grace.

Rejoice! You Qualify

Be glad you qualify for Him and His grace by being the sinner and failure you are. Celebrate that you can cast yourself on Him and His acceptance through His shed blood. Rest in the assurance that He wants to be the merciful supply of all you ever really need.

Don't expect in this life ever to be able fully to obey the royal law of love any more than the Pharisees could. Cast yourself on Him who alone can love fully and freely because He *is* love. Begin to learn to let Him live and love through you. This isn't as difficult as you might think, because He is in you and you are in Him.

The alternative is to keep on as you have in the past. Pridefully ashamed of our sin, we've tried to hide from it and from Him, just as Adam and Eve did after their first sin.

Instead, be honest with Him. Bring your sin and failure to Him. Let Him deal with it. Find Him to be trustworthy, even in handling your weaknesses. Find out He keeps His commitment to be all you need as you simply resign everything to Him, resting yourself in Him and His ability in you.

Everything's Out of Whack

"But, everything in my world seems out of joint," you say. "So it isn't going to work like you claim it will."

First, I didn't claim *it* would work. Only Jesus works—nothing less and nothing else.

Second, everything is going to be out of whack as long as we're in a sinning world. You'd better let God teach you to live at peace with this loathsome reality, or you'll never live at peace in this world. We simply must stop living in a world of pretense. We have to become real with God, with ourselves, and with our world.

Third, how can we live at peace in a world gone askew? The only way is that He must replace this world as our environment. *"In Him we live and move and have our being"* (Acts 17:28). We were made for perfection, not for this sinning world which is the opposite of perfection. May the perfect God increasingly become our environment.

Further, God *"chose us in Him before the foundation of the world, that we should be holy and without blame before Him in love"* (Ephesians 1:4). There's no need to grovel, then, in our failure and sin. Instead we can live in holy

17

excitement that all the perfect righteousness of our lovely Lord Jesus Christ has been credited to our account. We can stand blameless before the Judge of all the universe, who also happens to be our loving heavenly Father. In His Son's perfect righteousness, we stand before God positionally blameless, as we shall finally be in practice.

Enjoy Being in Him

Through the rest of this book, I'll be trying to help you learn how to live at home *in Him* who is also *in you*—in Him who is the perfectly satisfying environment God has prepared for us for all of time and eternity. I'll try to help you spend the rest of your life enjoying your position in Him.

But let me warn you first. The flesh, your old independent self, will do its best to prevent you from allowing the Lord to be your center and circumference, your environment, and your very life. This independent self will do its best to keep itself at the center even of your finest attempts to rest contentedly in Him and His work for you.

CHAPTER 2

Oh, To Be Needy

*Unless you are converted [turned around]
and become as little children, you will
by no means enter the kingdom of heaven.
Therefore whoever humbles himself
as this little child is greatest in the kingdom
of heaven.*
—Matthew 18:3-4

Our hope for a Christianity that really works doesn't lie in our achievements. Instead it lies in our willingness to recognize our sin, failure, and inability and to admit our neediness.

The beauty of this is that we all qualify. None of us is left out! If we can only see it, then we can acknowledge we're all very needy.

God's Principles Are So Different

Now, it's beginning to become quite clear, I hope, that the principles of the kingdom of God are opposite from those of this present evil world. However, we may not yet recognize just how difficult it is to forsake the ideas of this world for those of the one to come. We naturally assume, for instance, that success is success, and weakness and need are the opposite of success. So Paul's statement in 1 Corinthians 12:10 that when he was weak, then he was strong, seems not only contradictory, but foolish.

Nothing Else Works!

Few of us feel that our Christianity works as we'd like it to. Instead we live in a recurring cycle of failure that goes something like this:

We fail!

We let God down!

We feel guilty!

We run from God!

How does this pattern affect us? We are left in a recurring, or perhaps even in a continual, state of practical separation from the Lord. We then find ourselves in a nearly constant cycle of disappointment, loneliness, hurt, frustration, and anger, which we try to cover up with a pretense that this pattern isn't so. In turn, the denial leaves us feeling we are hypocritical and dishonest with ourselves, the Lord, and, of course, others.

I know this is not a pretty picture, and perhaps you'd rather not see it. If in some measure it fits you, let me assure you there's something better for you. There isn't merely hope. There's more. There's love, joy, and deep peace that surpasses human understanding. Best of all, there is God Himself for you!

Daddy Cares!

The last thing I want to encourage is disrespect for almighty God. Our God is omniscient, omnipresent, omnipotent, perfect, infinite, eternal, holy, pure, just, good, true, faithful, loving, and kind. He is the alpha and omega, the beginning and the end. He is unchanging. He is majestic with a glory that human eyes can't stand to look upon. Mere words can't begin to describe His perfection, beauty, and wonder. We must stand in awe.

But this wondrous Person is my Father, my Papa, my Daddy. Paul says so in Romans 8:15. It is by His Spirit that we cry, *"Abba [Papa], Father."*

I fear we've missed the most significant point of Jesus' teaching about our need to come to God as little children. He said: *"Unless you are converted [turned around], and become as little children, you will by no means enter the kingdom of heaven. Therefore whoever humbles himself as this little child is greatest in the kingdom of heaven"* (Matthew 18:3-4).

Tell me, what is the one certain thing about children? Surely, it is that they are dependent on their parents, whether they willingly recognize it or not.

What do we need to turn from more than anything else? Surely, it is our desire to be independent, to run our lives without interference from anyone, including almighty God.

One evening our granddaughter was "on her high horse." When she's like that, she is headed for trouble. So big four-year-old that she was at the time, I picked her up, laid her down in my arms, and tried to cuddle her. It was no use. She wanted no part of it. She wanted her stubborn, willful independence, so she simply could not accept my love.

Does that remind you of anyone you know?

Into the Waiting Arms

I was on the phone with a lady I had once counseled regularly for many months. I was offering new counsel. She interrupted me to say, "I remember you telling me to just lay myself down in the arms of God, and I do it!"

Regardless of the circumstances, you need to run to your Father and throw yourself into His arms of love. Whether you have failed and want to run away from God, or you are being tempted, or you are frightened, worried, anxious, or you are just trying to make it on your own, simply run into the waiting arms of Love —that is your hope.

The Curse of Independence

We've been taught that life has no value or meaning apart from freedom. We've been taught that this freedom is found only in independence. We've been taught a lie. At least in the spiritual dimension, our only hope and freedom is in dependence on our Father God.

What gets our children into so much trouble? Surely, it is just this cursed spirit of independence. Let my child trust me and depend on me to help, and then I can help. Let him not, and there's little I can do for him.

God help us to hate our cursed spirit of independence, our insistence on trying to do it all ourselves. Paul reminds us in 2 Corinthians 3:5 that we are not *"sufficient of ourselves to think of anything as being from ourselves, but our sufficiency is from God."*

I remember so well one day soon after the Lord began specially drawing me to Himself. I was turning off the parkway near my office when I was startled with the awful realization that I really didn't want to depend on the Lord. I wanted my independence. This was a shock indeed for one who had dedicated his life to the Lord thirty-eight years earlier!

Oh, To Be Needy

Start out simply recognizing you must be made needy enough to run into the arms of Love. Know that it's your role to be needy enough to turn to the Lord in every circumstance. Accept your need to be needy enough always to depend on Him, not on yourself, for whatever it is you need, for all you need. Long for the Lord to make you needy enough to despise the spirit of independence that plagues you.

Take the first step forward. Let the Lord do what He must to bring you to the place of being needy enough to need much time alone with Him. He'll teach you to realize again and again your neediness and to recognize your rebellious spirit of independence that wants not to acknowledge your need.

Can You Believe It?

As I was editing this manuscript, suddenly I felt, "Oops, people aren't going to like to be needy, dependent, hungry, and humble. They'll see no fun in that! It sounds downright awful!"

That idea came as a terrible shock to me. Since the Lord has broken my rebel spirit, some of my sweetest times have been alone with Him being needy, dependent, hungry, and humbled before Him. That is real fun, real joy, real happiness. It's the wonderful beginning of the delightful Christianity that really works.

Whatever your fears, they aren't justified. Walking with God in humble, dependent neediness of spirit is the most excitingly wonderful thing in the world.

Recall that inspiring thought from the first chapter: you don't have to grovel when you see your failure. Rather, let God teach you to view your failure as your hope. Let Him teach you to see it as a call to run into the forgiving, loving, caring arms of your Father God. There receive His love and whatever else you need, including both the willingness and the capacity to become poor and needy before Him so that He might become your everything.

Be glad when He uses your failure to show you your neediness and the folly of your independence. Your self-dependence leads only to spiritual failure and despair. It is hardly the thing to hold onto.

A New Spirit

> *Blessed are the poor in spirit,*
> *for theirs is the kingdom of heaven.*
> *Blessed are those who mourn,*
> *for they shall be comforted.*
> *Blessed are the meek,*
> *for they shall inherit the earth.*

Blessed are those who hunger and thirst
for righteousness,
for they shall be filled.
—Matthew 5:3-6

I am the vine, you are the branches:
He who abides in Me, and I in him,
bears much fruit;
for without Me you can do nothing.
—John 15:5

My dear friend, perhaps this isn't where you wanted to start your quest to come close to the Lord in a Christianity that really works, but sooner or later you'll have to start here. There is no place else to start.

CHAPTER 3

Oh, To Be Dependent

> LORD, my heart is not haughty,
> nor my eyes lofty. Neither do I concern myself
> with great matters,
> nor with things too profound for me.
> Surely I have calmed and quieted my soul,
> like a weaned child with his mother:
> like a weaned child is my soul within me.
> —Psalm 131:1-2

When we recognize how needy we really are, why do we still try to live the Christian life as though it were possible for *us* to do so? Because we honestly believe it is. We really don't believe our Lord's word, *"Without Me, you can do nothing"* (John 15:5).

We're prone to quote, *"The heart is deceitful above all things, and desperately wicked; who can know it?"* (Jeremiah 17:9), without knowing it. The doctrine of the depravity of man is widely accepted among God's people. Still we seem to have little conception of its impact on our daily lives as born-again Christians.

We Simply Don't Have It!

No one is good but One, that is, God.
   —Matthew 19:17

We have *nothing* good in ourselves. Not now. Not ever. We're dependent on the Lord always for every good thing, whether we like it or not. We have no choice!

Many of us have memorized Romans 12:1-2 with its call to let God have our lives to transform them into His image. Few make any connection with the prior verse in Romans 11:36, *"For of Him and through Him and to Him are all things, to whom be glory forever"* (Romans 11:36). We have missed the impact of the words, *"All things were made through Him, and without Him nothing was made that was made"* (John 1:3). We don't seem to realize the truth hasn't changed: anything good that gets done only occurs because God does it.

Wonderfully Dependent on Him

Can you imagine it? Really? He offers *Himself* to you. The God of all the universe, the One who spoke the worlds into existence and created the tiniest microbe, offers Himself to you in love, to provide for every need you have. He gives Himself to you to depend on for everything. Can you dream in your most incredible dreams of anything half as good or half as great?

He Is Our Life and Hope

Our Lord asserts, *"No one is good but One, that is, God"* (Luke 18:19). But we don't want to know that this includes us! We can say the words easily enough, but somehow their meaning eludes us.

Paul addressed this issue when he said, *"I have been crucified with Christ; it is no longer I who live, but Christ lives in me; and the life which I now live in the flesh I live by the faith in the Son of God, who loved me and gave Himself for me"* (Galatians 2:20). Only Christ can live the Christian life; we cannot. To try is to live in futility, frustration, and failure.

When God gave us His salvation and His righteousness as a free gift, He didn't give it separate from the Savior. It is Christ Himself given unto us. Now, living in us, Christ *"is made unto us wisdom, and righteousness, and sanctification, and redemption"* (1 Corinthians 1:30 KJV). He is waiting and longing to be all we need. We simply must become humble, admit our need, and depend on Him to be our supply.

"Christ in you, the hope of glory" (Colossians 1:27). He is our only hope for living the Christian life.

We've Got a Problem

We may not see His willingness to live His life through us as the delightful offer from our tender Father God and our gracious Savior that it is. Instead, strange as we are, we tend to see it as a threat to our independence. Can you believe it? God taking away our deadly existence to give us His perfect, infinite life is a threat?

Paul candidly admitted, *"I know that in me (that is, in my flesh) nothing good dwells"* (Romans 7:18). Still looking for a way to save our self-life, we may say, "That's it. Only in our flesh is there no good thing." You're right, my friend, but I recommend you take out that word, *only*.

Let the emphasis be reversed. All in us is of the flesh that isn't of the Spirit, who so wonderfully dwells in us. Only He within us is good and does good, is righteous and does righteousness. We need to accept His word on it and gladly leave it at that.

But, somehow, as incredible as it may be, I may still let the evil one convince me I'm getting a bad bargain! Let's get this straight once and for all. We have no good thing in ourselves. We're dependent on the Lord right now and always for every good thing, whether we like it or not. We have no choice.

He has given us Himself to dwell in us richly. In everything we do, say, and think, we have the right, the privilege, and the need to depend on Him, His power, His authority, His resources of whatever we need now, right now. He is ours, and so are all His resources.

We Prefer Our Independence

Our rebel selves prefer to depend on their puny resources in place of His omnipotent, omniscient, infinitely perfect, perfectly infinite resources. Old Testament Israel was destroyed because of this same awful, degrading, destructive spirit of independence. The Lord said through Isaiah:

You are wearied in the length of your way;
yet you did not say, "There is no hope."
You have found the life of your [own] hand;
therefore, you were not grieved.
I will declare your righteousness
and your works; for they will not profit you.
When you cry out, let your collection of idols
[your own resources] deliver you;
but the wind will carry them all away,
a breath will take them.
but he who puts his trust in Me
shall possess the land,
and shall inherit My holy mountain.
—Isaiah 57:10, 12-13

Becoming dependent on the Lord for everything, including our spiritual lives and development, cuts against the grain of the flesh —our independent selves. We not only don't want it, we positively reject it. But our resources aren't only puny, especially when it comes to spiritual matters, they're non-existent. Worse, they're destructive!

Hopelessness Is the Beginning of Hope

It would be well for us to ask ourselves often, "Is my attitude right now one of willing dependence on almighty God for all things?"

Perhaps your answer leaves you discouraged, bordering even on the hopeless. That's the perfect place to start!

But if you've read this far, and you still think you're all right, then you're in trouble. If this is your case, you need to find out if you really know the Lord as your Savior from sin. If you don't, tell Him you need Him now and receive Him as your own personal Savior. If you do know Him, ask Him to show you your continuing sin and need of Him.

Much to our displeasure, God often uses life's difficult circumstances to bring us to see our sin and need. Through these, He seeks to tear us from our natural self-reliance. He wants to make us willingly dependent on Him, our all-sufficient God and Savior.

A New Prayer

It is vital that you stop trying to escape whatever makes you more dependent on the Lord. Instead, ask the Lord to teach you to look to Him for the willingness to accept whatever He sends to help drive you to Himself.

An unusual aspect of my own story began nearly twenty-five years before I started seriously responding to God's drawing. I can recall it so vividly. As I was driving along the St. Lawrence River, I asked the Lord to give me a break. As a youth leader, I'd faced trials I hadn't anticipated and was deeply hurt by older pastors and leaders.

For the next seven years, God granted my request. Finally, I told Him He was free to put the heat back on, doing whatever it would take to draw me to Himself. Little did I know what I asked. Little did I recognize the hardness of my heart and what it would take to break me.

Throughout the constant trials of the next twenty years, I asked Him not to take the heat off until He'd accomplished His purposes in my life. He didn't, nor has He yet, though the circumstances have changed. I give Him praise that He loves me so much.

Recently our distress from my wife's Parkinsonism and other difficulties was such that I started asking the Lord to take the heat off again. Realizing what I asked, I recanted and told Him whatever He needed to do in my life was alright. In His love, He sent some relief anyway.

Unusual Advice

For several years I have developed the practice of collecting the correspondence from hurting people who write the ministry and then spending a few hours phoning them. On one occasion, I called a young wife and mother who had written that she didn't know if there was any use seeking the Lord, as it didn't seem to get her anywhere. I came to find out, she was quite sporadic in seeking Him. Still, I didn't emphasize the need of such consistency.

Instead, I asked whether she was willing to let Him do whatever He needed to make her willing to allow His transforming work. She honestly admitted her fear of the idea. Acknowledging that it was bound to be scary, I said, "It's for only a short time. From it you, your family, and perhaps countless others stand to benefit for an infinite time. It's simply a wise investment."

Be willing to let God enable you to accomplish the humanly impossible—even to be grateful that He sends trials to purge you and draw you to Himself. Let your prayer not be for premature deliverance, but that He would teach you to need Him, trust Him, love Him, lean on Him, depend on Him, run to Him, and throw yourself into His arms of love. Pray that He will teach you to live in vital union with Him, and from Him receive all you need for life and godliness.

Willingness

I know how impossible this may seem, but you can start toward this goal right now by simply resigning yourself and all of your reservations to the Lord. Just give yourself and your future to the God and Savior who wants to carry you in His arms of love all the day long.

Now, let me warn you of the ever-present danger that we may feel we are somehow earning His love and acceptance. Our willingness to be needy and dependent does not merit His love, nor does it earn our deliverance. Never! Our neediness and dependency represent our failure, which qualifies us for His success. But it is our failure and His success—nothing can change this. We must not let the world, the flesh, the devil, or all three in concert deceive us.

Our hopeless failure is the beginning of hope in Him. His victory in us is in our defeat. His life in us is fully realized in our death. Hold this wondrous truth in your heart. Thank God for all that reveals your hopelessness and that drives you to have hope in Him alone.

Too Much to Ask?

Will you trust Him enough to let Him do whatever He must in your life so He can give you all the love He longs to give you? If that's too much to ask, my heart aches for you because of what you're so pitifully denying yourself.

It aches, too, for my lovely Lord, because He so longs to give you His love and receive it back from you. And you're denying Him what He wants, perhaps, more than anything else.

As we continue together, you'll learn how intensely trustworthy our God really is. But if you've learned to mistrust Him as you have people, it will take a while for you to learn how wrong you've been.

So just go on. Put your hand in His. Let Him lead you and show you how much He loves you and how much He really is to be trusted.

CHAPTER 4

None But the Humble Heart

The sacrifices of God are a broken spirit,
a broken and a contrite heart;
These, O God, You will not despise.
—Psalm 51:17

But on this one will I look: on him
who is poor and of a contrite spirit,
and trembles at My word.
—Isaiah 66:2

What is a sure essential to a Christianity that really works? How do we get close to the heart of God? What is the one thing without which there is no real personal revival? Let God Himself answer in these words:

For thus says the High and Lofty One
Who inhabits eternity,
whose name is Holy;
I dwell in the high and holy place,
with him who has
a contrite and humble spirit,

> *to revive the spirit of the humble,*
> *and to revive the heart of the contrite ones.*
> *—Isaiah 57:15*

> *The LORD is near those*
> *who have a broken heart;*
> *and saves such as have a contrite spirit.*
> *—Psalm 34:18*

This book is intended to be a manual for living in continuous revival. What is revival?

Spiritual revival is not confession of sin, as much as that may be in evidence. Spiritual revival is not even inner conviction of sin or external evidence of grief for sin, as potent a reality as these may be. Spiritual revival is not even changed lives or changed communities.

The *sine quo non* of revival, that without which it does not exist, is a humbling of the human heart and spirit before almighty God. If you won't let God humble you, no vital, close dynamic relationship with God is available to you! You can spend as many hours in prayer as you might or run yourself ragged serving others, but without a contrite heart, no Christianity will really work for you.

What Is Revival Humility?

First, be assured revival humility is not something exclusively reserved for times of mass revival. Far from it, my dear Christian friend. Like every one of God's gifts of grace, you have a right to begin enjoying it right now and every moment of your Christian life.

Humility is not the end of all enjoyment, not a long face and a sad heart, and definitely not thinking self-depreciating thoughts. Rather, humility is simply agreeing with God about us.

How does God see His human creatures? He knows we need Him as our creator and as our sustainer. *"All things were created through Him and for Him; and He is before all things, and in Him all things consist [hold together],"* Colossians 1:16-17 informs us. We can't take one breath to sustain the next instant's life without His divine permission and enabling.

God sees Himself not only as our source and sustainer, but also as our reason for being. Colossians 1:16 says not only that all things were created by Him, but they were also created for Him: for His use, for His praise, and in our case, for His companionship.

Now, let's ask that question again: how does God view His human creation? Accurately. Precisely as we really are. Certainly not with the self-deluding, prideful view we have.

He sees us created in His own image to bring Himself praise, honor, and glory. He sees us with this glorious image terribly marred by sin. He sees this sin as the stuff of which destruction and death are made, as the awful plague and abomination it is. Moreover, He sees sin actually put to death and destroyed at the cross positionally. As we walk in Him, denying ourselves and rejecting our self-dependence, it's put to death in practice, too.

He sees the potential for the restoration of His own image in mankind by His indwelling presence. He sees the potential for eternal good produced by Him and His mighty life in us to His eternal praise, honor, and glory. He sees the possibility of growing fellowship between Himself and this once-corrupted human creation. He sees it all being accomplished by His own initiative and His own dynamic—His life lived in ours—and none of it as the result of independent human effort. Rather, He knows that is prideful and counter-productive.

To See As He Does

What is it that stops us from seeing ourselves and God as He does? Pride! Pride becomes the unforgivable sin if allowed to continue. Nothing good is in that prideful independence from God that keeps us isolated, separated, and desolated apart from Him.

Pride consistently chooses its own perverse and destructive way in preference to the good and perfect way of God. No words can fully describe its ignorance, blindness, stupidity, and folly; nor yet the eternal death, damnation, and destruction that are both the stuff of which it is made and its natural end result.

How we need to be humbly thanking God for His undeserved mercy and grace. Our pride would lift us up, instead, to steal from that eternally glorious, gracious God something of His honor and appropriate it to ourselves in all our impurity, imperfection, and degradation. Let us praise Him always for the amazing availability of His forgiveness even of such unfathomable insolence!

Living in Delusion

All our lives we've been living in awful delusion. As a result, we've been terribly cheated. Pridefully looking to and depending on our helpless selves rather than our completely capable God, we've been constantly short-changed. Our rebellion has isolated us from righteousness, peace, joy, and our one true Love. It has robbed us of the gentleness and goodness that alone can make life a pleasure.

But we have no ability to do anything about it. Real revival humility is the simple recognition of your inability and God's ability.

Now, if you think you can develop your humility by trying, go ahead. When you are sick of having fallen for the same old lie again, return to the Father, ask His forgiveness, and trust Him to give you His humility. After all,

41

you've been granted access to God and all He is and has by the blood of Christ. Come to Him in no merit but His. Rest in your established place of union with Him, knowing that He is working humility in you for His glory.

Let me assure you that, as poorly as you may do this, God will be pleased with even your most feeble response to His love. He'll begin to make real to you something of these heretofore misty realities. He'll begin to become more precious and all in opposition to Him despicable. This will be the humbling of your heart and spirit in revival humility.

How She Hurt

That dear lady phoned again, distraught. Appreciating me as she did, she still couldn't listen to my responses to her hurting heart. She was angry! God had let her down. For a couple of months she'd been ill. During that time the Lord had answered her prayer to bring her temper under control. Now she was feeling better, but the anger had returned. She'd feared this would happen, and it had.

I told her that, instead of being angry with the Lord, she needed to be thankful that even for a while her prayer had been answered. She had been free of her awful stifling, destructive anger. The Lord loved her and understood both her desire to be rid of the anger and her moral incapacity to rid herself of it.

God didn't have it in for her. Neither had He abandoned her. He was concerned for her. She didn't have to earn His love by her good works. He knew she was a sinner and only expected anything better of Him in her, not of herself. She could trust Him to deliver her in His time and way as he taught her to rest contently in her place at home in Him.

I described what I'd do if given the right to choose for her. One choice was to be rid of her sin of anger and, as a result, swell up in pride and independence from God at her achievement. Already, she had proved this was a real possibility by the return of her anger as soon as she was no longer so dependent on the Lord. The other choice was to let God show her need of Him by allowing her to succumb to her anger and so humbling her and teaching her really to depend on Him. I'd choose the latter.

God wasn't being so hard on her after all. Perhaps He knew that pride is a far more destructive sin than anger. It isolates us from God more than does anything else, because by it we choose to be arrogantly independent from Him.

"Trust Him" was my advise to her. "Trust His life in you, His ability in you, His timing. Don't try to overcome in your own strength, or you'll be worse off living in supposed success and paralyzing pride."

He always knows what's best for us! He works best in us when we trustfully leave Him undisturbed to do His work without our interference.

You Can Never Go Farther!

Be glad for His humbling work. Its benefits are without end. The psalmist says:

> *The meek will he teach his way.*
> *—Psalm 25:9 KJV*

As you seek to walk with God in a Christianity that really works, you'll realize repeatedly your need of His teaching. You'll never get beyond it. Many times you'll think He's taking you back to square one. In a sense, He will be. You can never get beyond the basic spiritual and relational realities.

You'll find that He can only teach those who are humble, meek, teachable. You'll discover that quite often what He is teaching you again is humility or meekness of spirit.

A meek and quiet spirit is treasured by God because it is incorruptible, eternal. In it there is nothing of corruption. Communing with God is only possible in a meek and quiet spirit. You can never go further, higher, or deeper with God than going lower and still lower in quiet, humble meekness.

CHAPTER 5

None But the Hungry Heart

*Blessed are those who hunger and thirst
for righteousness;
for they shall be filled.*
—*Matthew 5:6*

*Because you say, "I am rich,
have become wealthy,
and have need of nothing,"
and do not know that you are wretched,
miserable, poor, blind, and naked.*
—*Revelation 3:17*

May we become genuinely needy in our hearts and spirits, and may this neediness lead us straight to the source of supply, our almighty God. May we be humbled to acknowledge our need of the Lord alone, our hope, our life, our all. May we invite Him to produce in us a spirit that is truly dependent, reliant on Him for all we need. May our hearts be open to receive His gifts of love, especially Himself.

Oh, To Be Hungry

How pathetic is that picture of our lovely Lord as He stands outside the closed door of His church, meekly knocking for admittance. This is the Creator of all the universe who, loving and lowly, sacrificed Himself to redeem us at such awesome cost. Outside the church door, he calls to those within who haven't eaten so much of this world's husks that they have no hunger left for Him:

Behold, I stand at the door and knock.
If anyone hears My voice and opens the door,
I will come in to him
and dine with him, and he with me.
—Revelation 3:20

Quick fix, big thrill, power-hungry Christianity has been in vogue. God's people have preferred showmanship to genuine spiritual power, instant gratification to the slow-growing fruit of the Spirit. Look around you at the results.

The fruit of the Spirit grows with exposure to the sunlight of God's love and to the rain of divinely permitted trials. As we spend time in communion with Him in humility of spirit and allow Him to use trials and tribulations to turn us sweetly to Him from the still-present sin and self, his fruit in us matures.

Hungering for Him

Within us is a holy hunger for our gracious, wonderful God. This hunger was placed there by the Spirit when He came to dwell in our spirits when we first received Christ as our Savior. But, most of us haven't been in the habit of adequately feeding that hunger for Him. Many of us have been starving our spiritual longings after the Lord.

Let me ask you: how much of your praying is for the things of this life and how much for the next? Do you ever take time just to love, worship, and adore your lovely Lord? Do you take time to see Him as He is in all His wonder and glory, in all His perfection and beauty, in all His grace and mercy, in all His kindness and love? Do you take time to meditate on His magnificent perfection?

I don't blame folks too much for their wrong praying. You see, if you look around in the Lord's church, it's hard to find anyone who sets an example. To learn without good models to copy is very difficult.

Who, *Me?*

Let me challenge you, then, to become an example for others to follow. "Who, *me?*" you yelp. Yes, *you!* No matter how unspiritual, how much of a failure you feel. In fact, just because you feel so unspiritual, such a failure, you qualify. Others need to learn from just such a model as you who can admit to being needy.

Jesus said in the great *Sermon on the Mount* that blessed are the poor in spirit, the mourners, the meek, the hungry, the thirsty. You qualify only as you realize something of just how poor, how mournful, how hungry, and how thirsty you really are. So take in hand the little sense of neediness you have, thank God in your heart that He has given you even that little bit, and go to Him.

As you look to Him, little by little He will increase that small sense of neediness. At length you may come even to glory in the very neediness that once frightened you so. Ultimately you may see yourself in Him, resting and remaining there, content for Him in you to satisfy all your needs.

An Appetizer

Now, before I begin to lead you into the way this can come about, let me whet your appetite a little. Listen to David, that sweet singer of Israel, a man after God's own heart. Let his words sink deep into your heart. Let them begin to induce in you a perhaps unfamiliar response to your lovely Lord's longing love for you.

For He satisfies the longing soul,
and fills the hungry soul with goodness.
...Let the hearts of those rejoice
who seek the LORD.
Seek the LORD and His strength;
seek his face evermore.
...The young lions lack and suffer hunger;
but those who seek the LORD shall not
lack any good thing.
...I sought the LORD, and He heard me,
and delivered me from all my fears.
...The poor shall eat and be satisfied;
Those who seek Him will praise the LORD.
...My heart and my flesh cry out
for the living God.
...O God, You are my God;
early will I seek You; my soul thirsts for You;
my flesh longs for You
in a dry and thirsty land,
where there is no water.
...As the deer pants for the water brooks,
so pants my soul for You, O God.
My soul thirsts for God, for the living God.
When shall I come and appear before God?
—Selections from the Psalms

The answer to this question, *"When shall I come and appear before God?"* is, "Any time I will!" Yet we take such sparse advantage of this wonderful privilege of appearing before the omnipotent God of all the universe. What fools we mortals are.

This God of love promises us: *"You will seek Me and find Me, when you search for Me with all your heart"* (Jeremiah 29:13). His perfectly spotless Son, our Savior and our God, often found it wise to retire from the pressing crowd. In *"the mountain"* or *"a place apart,"* He would hold sacred conversations with His Father.

Our quick "gimmee" prayers grieve the God of love who longs to fellowship with us in the intimacy of exchanged love. The psalmist king was a man after God's own heart just because nothing was, or ever could be for long, as important as his intimacy with God. He said:

One thing I have desired of the LORD,
that will I seek:
That I may dwell in the house of the LORD
all the days of my life,
to behold the beauty of the LORD,
and to inquire in His temple.
—Psalm 27:4

Oh, may we seek Him so. May He become adorable to us. May His beauty draw us to Himself in the longing of love so nothing else but He can fill our growing hunger for Himself.

CHAPTER 6

God Is All We Need

For of Him and through Him and to Him,
are all things,
to whom be glory forever. Amen.
—Romans 11:36

Even to gray hairs I will carry you!
I have made [you], and I will bear [you];
even I will carry [you], and will deliver you.
—Isaiah 46.4

Hopefully we have begun to see how essential it is for us to be needy, dependent, humble, and hungry toward our God. We need to pursue the question: how is our need to be met, our hunger satisfied? How are we to get close to the heart of God as we long to? How does this Christianity that works function?

Even though every true child of God wants to be close to the Lord deep inside, one of the great disappointments for most Christians has been the lack of that intimacy. Why is this?

Unfortunately, to say we want to be close to Him isn't to say we are responding to the wooing of the blessed Spirit as we ought. In fact, most of the Lord's dear ones have long since given up any idea they ever had of really being close to Him. They feel it just hasn't worked. They're deeply disappointed, hurt, and—if the truth were known—angry.

Substitutes for God

We've largely substituted something less than God Himself for our aim. Ask yourself, "How are we generally expected to live the Christian life, grow in grace, know our Lord, have Christian victory?" Three common answers come to my mind immediately: obedience to external commands, correct doctrine, and religious experiences. Legalism, doctrinalism, and experientialism have probably touched all believers at some point in their Christian walk.

No matter what helpful instantaneous experiences may be ours, the relationship we seek with our Lord is a continual development, a moment-by-moment spiritual transformation. It's not a once-in-a-lifetime experience, nor is it arrived at through simply believing or even acting on biblical truth. As for external self-disciplines, self-denial, and self-imposed external obedience, only disappointment awaits those who expect these to be adequate to lead them into dynamic spiritual living.

None of these substitutes for God, nor any others we manufacture, will ever satisfy the hunger in our needy hearts for God Himself. None of them will ever provide a Christianity that really works.

Not by Works

God's commands are to be fully obeyed. Correct doctrine is not inconsequential. Valid Christian experiences do occur. However, many of us have allowed these to replace the Lord Himself as our hope. In New Testament terms, this amounts to legalism or fleshly works.

In his epistles, Paul had to give special attention to correcting this spiritual aberration. (See Galatians 3:1-5 and Philippians 3:3.) From the little attention given it today, one would think it scarcely poses any danger to us. In fact, however, it characterizes the carnal church in our day just as disastrously as it did in Paul's.

The Lord Our Hope

Now, we've already said it repeatedly and will continue to do so. Only our wonderful Lord Himself is our hope, as He is our life and our all. (See Colossians 1:27; 3:4, 11; 1 Timothy 1:1; Romans 15:13.) This is the one reality of overriding importance to all Christians.

Whatever it is we need must be received from no other source than the Mighty One Himself. After all, He is all we need.

To look to any other source is idolatry, which is the worst sin against our God. Yet it has been possessively and obsessively ours since our birth. We're so accustomed to it that it seems natural and even comfortable, like an old shoe. We may find it difficult to recognize the very limited extent to which we abandoned it when we came to Christ for eternal salvation from our sin, its guilt, and punishment. We've still a long way to go.

Who Is Your God?

When we declare this wonderful reality— that God Himself is all we need—we may be lampooned as trite and simplistic. That accusation may prove to be correct unless we show how He actually becomes our life and all in daily practice, and unless those of us who proclaim Him alone begin showing Him in our daily walk to be genuinely all we need.

For this to happen requires that we have a new God! Now, please forgive me for this overstatement. But there's a sense in which it really is so. We need to see our God as He is, not as we've been seeing Him. When our view of Him has been corrected, we'll have quite a different God than we had before.

So many of us view Him like the law really is, a hard taskmaster. Instead, He's our loving heavenly Father, always there for us, to soothe the hurt, to bind the wound, to encourage, and to uplift. He's always there loving, caring, giving, helping; He is eternally present not to condemn, but to transform.

Our condemnation was placed on our lovely Lord Jesus Christ at the cross. *"There is therefore now no condemnation to those who are in Christ Jesus"* (Romans 8:1). The Christian is freed from condemnation for sin through the finished work of Jesus Christ alone. But we insist that we get in on the act, that somehow our acceptance with God depends at least in part on us.

Is This You?

A long-time supporter of the ministry had written, "Please pray for me finally to break through this barrier which keeps me from having a personal relationship with God." Now, I couldn't stand the idea that this hurting heart was feeling shut out from God, so I called her. After I got an idea of her problem, I read her the whole first chapter of this manuscript!

How appreciative she was. She cried almost the whole time we'd talked. Her God had always been angry with her. She said, "I keep hearing, *'If I regard iniquity in my heart, the LORD will not hear me.'* I feel separated from God, and I wonder what use there is in spending all the time I do in prayer. I keep hearing, *'Be perfect as I am perfect.'* I know I'm anything but perfect. I listen to your tape about passionate love for the Lord, but I haven't any."

She didn't want to give up. She was desperately sincere. She was spending time trying to seek the Lord, but she was getting no place. She was in danger of sooner or later entirely giving up seeking the Lord if something didn't change!

How my heart aches for every one of God's dear children who find themselves in such a predicament. But, let me assure you, it isn't necessary. Not at all!

He Loves Us So Much, Nothing Is Too Much

Your God doesn't have it in for you: He has it all for you. Everything you need, He has for you. Better still, He Himself *is* it for you. He *is* all you need.

God is not the source of your condemnation, but of your supply. He is even the source of your approval—not the approval of your sin, but of you in Christ Jesus. This God of love, and forgiveness, and mercy, and grace, this God is your loving heavenly Father.

I asked that dear lady what she did when her children did wrong. She said, "I discipline them."

"Then what?" I asked.

Before I could get the question out, she was replying, "I love them." As I asked her if she thought the Lord is a poorer parent than she, the smiles were obvious through her tears, even across the miles.

I reminded her that the Father's love sent His only, perfect Son to suffer indescribable agony and shame for us. He sent Him to buy us back from eternal separation from Him to eternal fellowship with Him. What then can He be unwilling to do for us, to give to us? *"He who did not spare His own Son, but delivered Him up for us all, how shall He not with Him also freely give us all things?"* (Romans 8:32).

You Really Can Trust Him

You need to continue correcting the terribly distorted picture you may have of the Lord, especially to come to see Him as totally trustworthy. You must see Him as always having in mind your ultimate good in every circumstance He allows.

This dear one had to be willing to accept even what seemed to be His withholding of Himself from her. She had to be willing to see this experience, too, as part of His doing the very best for her.

We need to see Him as the One of infinite perfection beyond all that the human mind is able to comprehend or human imagination devise. We were created to honor, worship, and adore Him through time and eternity. When we begin to see Him even a little like He really is, we can't do otherwise than worship.

May He enable us to see Him increasingly as He is in all His wonder and glory. May we stand in awe of Him. May we joyfully repudiate all that is not of Him, that we might begin enjoying Him forever.

This was the appearance of the likeness
of the glory of the LORD.
So when I saw it, I fell upon my face,
and I heard a voice of One speaking.
—Ezekiel 1:28

I have heard of You by the hearing of the ear:
but now my eye sees You.
Therefore I abhor myself,
and repent in dust and ashes.
—Job 42:5-6

CHAPTER 7

The Way into the Heart of God

He who dwells in the secret place
of the Most High
shall abide under the shadow of the Almighty.
—Psalm 91:1

I wait for the LORD, my soul waits,
and in His word do I hope.
My soul waits for the LORD
more than those who watch for the morning.
—Psalm 130:5-6

Now, let's be sure we have our goal in clear focus. The Lord Himself is our hope. He is our objective, and even the way to that objective. (See Romans 11:36, Colossians 3:11, and John 14:6.) The Lord Himself—loving, giving, and sharing Himself as the essence of all we could ever ask or need—must be our aim.

Our part is simply to be at home in Him, responding to Him with calm, quiet hearts. In Him, He in us, we find ourselves being changed from within by His Spirit. We find ourselves becoming increasingly dependent, reliant, and receptive toward Him. This dependent spirit is evidenced by increasing abandonment to Him. Resulting in increasing trust and rest, meekness and quietness of spirit in Him, it leads to growing harmony and unity with Him and to the fruit of the Spirit being formed in us from which others may eat and live.

We may feel ourselves to be at an impossible distance from this goal. We may often feel we're making little or no progress toward it, wrongly assuming nothing good is happening just because we don't sense anything. In fact, God may sometimes be accomplishing most when He seems to be accomplishing nothing.

Let Him be in charge. Trust His working. Trust His promises. Trust His pace. Never give up looking to Him as your goal no matter how hopeless it may seem.

Now, how does a wonderful, practical, living relationship with our lovely Lord begin to develop and grow?

Our Relationship Is Already Established

The Spirit of God lives within us. We're His temples, His dwelling places. *"Christ in us"* is *"our hope of glory"* (Colossians 1:27). We are *"complete in Him"* (Colossians 2:10). He is in us, and we are in Him, as genuinely as ever will be (Ephesians 3:14-21). In other words, the relationship with God that we need was established in its essence the moment we received Christ Jesus as our Savior and became His. He Himself is gloriously present in us. We are wonderfully secure in Him. He is all we need.

So we don't run around looking for something we don't have. We remain content just being in Him, and He in us. We rest confident that Christ in us will increasingly fill and transform us. We rest more contentedly, more fully in Him, receiving ever more of His life for all our need, for all our life.

Our Way Opened

The way into the heart of God has been freely provided for every child of God by the blood of Christ shed in agony for us who are so unworthy (Hebrews 10:19)! He has established a genuine, open, and operative life-giving relationship with us. Through the blood-sprinkled way and our resultant position in Christ, our access is assured, our relationship established. We who are so unworthy can freely find in Him the satisfaction of our every need.

All we really need to do to experience the development of His life in us is to rest content in His love, peacefully at home there in Him. What a relief! Resting contentedly in the blessed assurance that He is in us, we are in Him is enough! As we rest there and stop interfering with His work, He'll freely draw us to Himself in love.

Spiritual Laziness

However, let us not assume that this resting in Him is an invitation to be spiritually lazy or unresponsive. Far from it! What is the point of His drawing us in love if we remain unresponsive to Him?

Our Lord draws us in many ways, and to them all He longs for us to respond. When at last we begin to rest in Him, delightedly conscious that we are in Him, He in us, and that's enough, we'll find our hearts long to be responsive to His drawings. This is the nature of the new heart He gives us.

Exercise yourself rather to godliness.
...Give attendance to reading,
to exhortation, to doctrine.
Do not neglect the gift that is in you,
...Meditate on these things;
give yourself entirely to them,
that your progress may be evident to all.
Take heed to yourself and to the doctrine.
Continue in them, for in doing this
you will save both yourself
and those who hear you.
—1 Timothy 4:7, 13-15

This Scripture isn't advocating the works of proud flesh. Rather, here we find some ways of responding in love to the good God who initiates every good thing in love.

God at Work!

Such a response to Him ought to be merely the evidence of His work within us. It ought to be the result of Him producing in us a desire to come to Him to live, walk, and rest contentedly at home in Him.

The glad response of the new man, created by God after the pattern of Christ Jesus, is a joyful abandonment to his loving God. The new man diligently and zealously responds by God's enabling to the inworking of His Spirit. Against all the combined efforts of the world, the flesh, and the devil to deter him, this new man simply cannot help inwardly longing for the Lord. He can't help longing for God in the new man, no matter how much outward appearances may claim he doesn't.

But watch out! The evil one will do his best to sell you a phony bill of goods right at this point. On the one hand, he will try to convince you that you can't be a child of God because you haven't this hunger for the Lord. If that doesn't work, He will do his best to convince you that seeking after the Lord is somehow unspiritual, a work of the flesh. He will try to catch you coming or going. Just give him no attention. Seek the Lord in spite of him and every fear He can generate in you.

Nothing Half-hearted

Let nothing deter you from your quest to come close to the heart of God, neither your place of rest in the Lord, nor the devil's tricks. Let there be nothing half-hearted about it. On the contrary, be willing to be obsessed with Jesus, Father God, and the Spirit—and to be maligned by those who aren't.

Ours must be a God-given intensity of spirit that demands that all else give way to the work God is doing in us. It must refuse to be derailed from seeking Him, the things of His realm of the eternal and spiritual, and His glory and praise. Ours must be a determination born within by the Spirit to know Him in glorious intimacy, a Spirit-born determination never to stop seeking Him, no matter the extent of our failure to find Him as we would like, a determination never to stop until He reveals Himself in us, us in Him, in present peace and joy in spite of the surrounding terror.

Who Is Going To Be Your God?

The world, the flesh, and the devil are the triumvirate god of this age. They have usurped the place and role of the almighty triune God as the god of mankind. To their call, man responds and offers his homage.

To our surprise and chagrin, this doesn't stop entirely when we're born again of God's Spirit. But it must stop. It must change. The question is: *how?*

How is this translated into practical God-approved, God-inspired, God-directed, God-empowered action? How is it translated into action neither dictated nor controlled by the old man of the flesh but by the new man of the Spirit in love? Where do we begin?

My failure to know and live the right answer to this question condemned me to thirty years of carnality as a minister of the gospel. The rest of the blame lay largely with my willful unyieldingness and my never getting to know anybody who lived close to the heart of God whose godly example I could follow.

Getting Acquainted

If then you were raised with Christ,
seek those things which are above, where
Christ is, sitting at the right hand of God.
Set your mind on things above,
not on things on the earth. For you died,
and your life is hidden with Christ in God.
—Colossians 3:1-3

Where do we begin? Upon the answer to this question, indeed, hangs everything. But, thank God, the answer is so very simple, even the youngest child of God can understand it.

Come to Jesus. Look as trustingly to Him as you may be able. Turn to Him from the attractions and distractions of life. Come to Him. Yield to your great Father God and Christ as much loving response to His drawing as He will enable.

Let Him teach you increasingly to see Him, know Him, worship Him, long after Him, praise Him, and fellowship with Him as He really is. Come to Him. As He teaches you how, come in rest and peace in Him rather than in destructive self-effort. That's all. Allow Him to teach you little by little to let go and let God.

A Conflict?

Let us therefore labor to enter into that rest.
—Hebrews 4:11 KJV

The meaning in the original is to make haste to enter into that rest. This labor of love is simple application of our hearts to come to Him in response to His call of love. We give ourselves diligently to responding and coming to rest in Him. There we get to know Him as He is and learn to relinquish everything that would detract from our doing so.

Why, then, do we have to endure so much instead of just entering into His rest? Because we don't come to Him as we ought in response to His love call, we don't learn to know Him as He is. Thus we fail to realize that we really can trust Him and rest securely in Him.

Our own self-centered attempts to come to rest in Him are so very unproductive—even counterproductive! Our underlying problem still is our resistance to Him—our inner, sometimes hidden, rebellion against Him. But why, after so long, are rebellion and resistance still so characteristic of us? Because we don't yet know Him in His love and truth, we cling to our misconceptions of Him.

This, then, is where we start: coming to Him and getting to know the true, loving Lord of the universe.

What things were gain to me,
those I have counted loss for Christ.
But indeed I also count all things loss
for the excellence of the knowledge
of Christ Jesus my LORD,
...that I may know Him.
—Philippians 3:7-8, 10

Focus on the Lord

He has been trying to get our loving, responsive attention all our lives. Let's at last begin to give it to Him in some little measure as He deserves it—to Him who gave Himself for us even to the awful death of the cursed cross. Let the focus of our interest go from ourselves to Him. After all, we're the problem. He's the solution!

Let God draw our attention lovingly to Himself and His things from the false triumvirate god: the world, the flesh, and the devil, and their things.

Who Is Incomparably More Important than *How*

How can our attention, our interest, our affection, be removed from this false god to the one true God? Our rebel hearts don't want to recognize that the answer is God Himself, nothing less and nothing other.

The *how* is the *Who*. We simply begin to look to, turn to, and come to God. Come for all you need, even for His enabling to refocus your attention, your interest, and your affection from yourself and the usurping triumvirate god of this age to the almighty triune God, Creator and Sustainer of all things.

Never Quit

Now, there's no need for you to follow any particular path I suggest to encourage this transition. Let God Himself be your teacher and guide as well as your objective. As I suggested in the introduction, let Him be uniquely yours.

But please, I beg you in the name of our loving Lord, start seeking Him today and don't ever forsake your quest. No other purpose in life is worthy of giving your maximum life-long concern. No other goal should so engage your attention. By comparison, all other objectives pale into insignificance.

Beware!

Be warned once more. The danger is ever-present, even if you are the most sincere seeker after God, that the focus of your attention will veer again and again from the Lord Himself. It shifts so readily from Him, not only to ourselves and our seen circumstances, but also to a means, a method, a concept, a doctrine, a feeling, or an approach to Him. God is not to be confused with anything less than Himself, not even with prayer or praise, worship or love, rest or peace. Our hope is in none of these. To settle for something less than the Lord—however delightful, helpful, or even necessary it may be—is to fail of our purpose entirely. Anything that stops short of Him, including the very road to Him, becomes no longer an asset, but a liability in the quest.

Failure to heed this warning may be one of the greatest deterrents to knowing the Lord in the practical intimacy that is your right as His child. My prayer is that God will enable us never to allow anything to deter us from seeking Him only, yielding to Him the loving, responsive attention He so seeks and deserves.

Know, also, that you respond to His drawing not for any benefit you or others may receive. Know it isn't even for your joy in being close to the heart of God, but only for His pleasure and because He alone is worthy!

Recall it again: anything I urge you to do is in danger of becoming a work of your independent self. Anything done as a human work is not only without merit, it is hurtful. Now, we'll never love the Lord and respond to Him as we ought. So we're in danger of trying hard to force ourselves to be loving and responsive to Him, to give Him our attention, to get to know Him. How horribly counterproductive that would be.

Giving God our attention properly, so we come to know Him ever more nearly as He is, is simply our spirit enlivened by His Spirit responding to His calling work. God alone initiates and empowers every good thing, including our giving Him our attention. Nothing is of you apart from Him, most assuredly not your loving, responsive attention to Him in meekness, rest, and peace.

However, having said this, let's remember that we're still in the flesh and we must start where we are. If we can't start trusting Him, looking to Him, getting to know Him, receiving from Him in meekness, rest, and peace, let's start as poorly as we must, allowing Him to make the needed changes in our responses. This, too, is His work.

To our own eternal harm, we've neglected our loving God. Isn't it time we changed?

"I Can't!"

True! You can't change. The sooner you learn you can't, the better. The sooner you realize it's for us to rest at home in Him, content that He in us is all we need for the accomplishment of any good goal, the better. But it's doubtful if even a few of us can start here. So let's start where we can by turning our attention to the Lord, who alone is able.

I have set the LORD always before me.
—Psalm 16:8

Your God Is Too Small

I was trying to awaken a man with some deep-seated emotional problems to his need of simply letting go and trusting God to look after the supposedly massive problems he thought he had. Suddenly, I burst out one day, "You've got a God that's too small and a you that's too big!"

Yes, he did, and so do we. So we always shall as long as we live here below. This will only significantly change as we trustingly yield to the Lord the loving, responsive attention He wants, so He can reveal Himself in His reality and fullness to us.

CHAPTER 8

Communication and Communion

O God, You are my God;
early will I seek You; my soul thirsts for You,
my flesh longs for You in a dry and thirsty
land, where there is no water;
so I have looked for You in the sanctuary,
to see Your power and Your glory.
Because Your lovingkindness is better than
life, my lips shall praise You.
Thus will I bless You while I live:
I will lift up my hands in Your name.
My soul shall be satisfied
as with marrow and fatness;
my mouth shall praise You with joyful lips.
When I remember You upon my bed,
I meditate on You in the night watches.
Because You have been my help,
therefore in the shadow of Your wings
I will rejoice.
My soul follows close behind You:
Your right hand upholds me.
—Psalm 63:1-8

As David discovered, God Himself needs to be the center and focus of our attention. Nothing else can take His place, not even prayer or communion with Him can be allowed to replace Him as our life-focus.

But tell me, will you please, how is the Lord to become increasingly real to us if not by some kind of communion with Him? How is He to get more and more of our attention and affection? Tell me, why do so many resist the idea that regular, consistent, extensive prayer communion with God is necessary if they're to grow in the Lord?

Twisted Out of Shape

For many of God's people, the real reason is that they have let their attention to that supplanting triumvirate god of this age continue to replace the loving attention due the triune God. We want to hold onto the things of this life—its possessions, pleasures and passions, its manners and methods, its hopes and helps.

We don't want to endure the revelation of our sin and sickness that is sure to come when our attention is really given to God. We don't care to hear the persistent demands of a God-awakened conscience that we repent and turn from our continuing rebellion. We don't want to spend our time with the God who can't even look on sin, especially not when there's so much sinful rebellion standing between us and Him that is unrepented of, unforsaken, and unforgiven.

We don't want to listen to the divine insistence that we find the eternal Creator and Sustainer of all things totally worthy of our trust. We don't want to believe He's entirely capable of caring for all our needs without our worry or interference.

We want to be able to complain at His management of our affairs. We want somehow to find an excuse for trying to get along without Him in everyday practice, even while professing Him as Lord and Master.

Don't Ask Too Much

We may be willing to admit the importance of prayer—provided it can be done on the fly. We may even allow for the desirability of an established regular time of daily devotions— provided it's a few quick moments that we can spend asking God to get us out of our problems and supply our needs and wants, after which we might list a few quick requests for others.

Now, we're quite willing to spend years preparing for a vocation. We'll invest seemingly endless hours learning to drive a car, operate a computer, get a degree we may not even need or use, or obtain a sales license of some kind. Once having obtained the goal, if we do really value our achievement, we recognize the need of continuing to exercise or improve our new-found skills.

Meanwhile, when it comes to spiritual concerns, we're not willing to give our loving God the time and attention a god deserves of his devotees, a master of his servants, a king of his subjects.

Taking God for Granted

We know a friendship has to be constantly cultivated, or it will die a natural death. We're well aware that historically engaged couples have spent a lot of time together laying a solid foundation for their developing relationship. We know the importance of husbands and wives enjoying pleasant times alone together —and the danger posed to the relationship where this isn't happening.

Yet we often act as though our love relationship with the Lord is just supposed to grow and develop automatically, without giving it or Him any special attention. We act as though we are to grow in His grace and have His victory over sin without willing, responsive participation on our part.

Can we draw close to the heart of God while we're ignoring Him, ignoring that infinitely perfect Person who offers us everything we can ever need, ignoring Him in favor of the garbage and husks of this world?

Dear Lord, forgive us.

Believe It!

The power of influence can't be measured. You will become like the person you are much with. The more you admire, respect, and love that person, the more you'll become like him.

So it is with being much with Christ. To start on your way to becoming more like Him may be as simple as this: be much with Him in loving communion, and be unconsciously changed into His likeness.

Finding Time

No matter how busy our schedules, we find time for the things we really enjoy and the things we absolutely have to do. For example, Hudson Taylor, the famed founder of what is now the Overseas Missionary Fellowship, found himself sleeping night after night in a room crowded with Chinese coworkers. There he was observed late into the night seeking the Lord and reading the Scriptures by a feeble light.

Here are some hints among which you may find help for your particular circumstances.

Recognize the urgency of finding a time. Dedicate yourself to finding the answer.

If you're really looking for an excuse not to spend time with the Lord, acknowledge it. Ask the Lord for a desire to be with Him. Set aside an appropriate time, and begin.

Go to bed much earlier than you're used to so you can get up before others will be up to disturb you. Don't use your spouse as an excuse. Go ahead without him or her.

If young children demand nearly full-time attention, put them all down for a rest at the same time. Close the doors and let them cry if you must. Believe it or not, eventually they'll get used to rest time and even enjoy it. How do you think workers at day care centers survive?

First thing in the morning is generally recognized to be best, but be prepared to take advantage of other times as the need demands or opportunity provides. Be prepared even to break up your sleep if necessary to work in your time with the Lord.

Wasted Hours, Wasted Hearts!

Instead of spending our time with the Lord, we too often waste our hours with TV, sports, the newspaper, unnecessary or even harmful books and magazines, and idle talk. We willingly forget that someday we'll answer to God for the gift of time as for all else He has given us that we so casually fritter away.

We fill our time, our minds, and ultimately our hearts with all but Him. Then we wonder why we're less responsive to Him than we would like and more responsive to the things of this world!

We should apply ourselves persistently both in prayer time and out to giving Him our attention, to meditating on Him, seeking for Him, longing after Him, seeing the center of our focus moved from ourselves and things of time and space to Him and things spiritual and eternal. But, by His enabling, it should be in quiet confidence in Him and His life in us that we give ourselves to seeking Him. When we find ourselves struggling forcibly by our independent selves to seek Him, we can back off, return to our quiet rest in Him, and let His almighty life in us take up the task.

Replacing Bad Attitudes

Whenever our attention turns to ourselves in prayer, we need to seek to be entirely open and honest with God about ourselves. As we do, we may realize our need of Him, our helplessness without Him, and the depravity of our hearts. Confession, repentance, and restitution will often result spontaneously. Though we may scarcely sense it to be so, His love will begin flowing out from us to Him and others.

Our self-centeredness and resistance to God, the circumstances He permits in our lives, or His will for us effectively divert the attention of the longing heart from the object of our love. It's this that needs to be abandoned as the appalling deterrent to true prayer communion with God in love that it is.

Our Awful Independent Spirits

This independent spirit may show up not only as sin and active resistance to God but as a negative reaction to people and difficult circumstances. This spirit has many different appearances, such as: a desire to remain in charge of our own circumstances, a mind or heart full of strife instead of peace, a preoccupation with the material world, or a long list of worries and concerns demanding our attention. It may even evidence itself as a barrage of needs with which we bombard God that all sound very right, even necessary and spiritual, but which are really concerns never rested with the Lord, submitted to His will, or entrusted to His care.

However it shows itself, this independent spirit is idolatry that effectively excludes primary attention to God even from our prayer time. Remember, the low, low doorway into

God's presence is to forsake all for Him and to Him. Let go of everything. Relinquish all to Him. Maintain no control over anything. Accept no primary responsibility for anything. Retain no ultimate ownership of anything. Tear down the idols. Have no real hope and no great need but Him. Just to have God in charge of all things for you is enough.

Expect Change

Each prayer time must be submitted to God's sovereign direction that His will may be done in it. We need to learn increasingly to accept what He sends our way in each time with Him without objection. Otherwise, we lose His peace, His joy, and His blessing.

At times we may seek Him earnestly, long after Him, want Him to be our all, eagerly pursue Him as the one great object and hope of our lives. At times we may worship, praise, and adore Him. Sometimes we may long to be able to love Him as we want to do. We may at one point want just to seek His honor and glory. At another we may want to wait on Him, look to Him quietly, meekly, attentively, receptively, dependently, expectantly. At still another we may want to rest in Him in love, resignation, and surrender.

As we look back, we may see that some of our seeking the Lord was quite tainted with proud flesh and its self-righteousness. We may wish so much that it had been otherwise. Still, isn't it better to risk this than never to begin? In fact, if we aren't content to start here, how could we ever start?

CHAPTER 9

Practical Prayer Hints

*As the deer pants for the water brooks,
so pants my soul for You, O God.
My soul thirsts for God, for the living God.
When shall I come and appear before God?*
—Psalm 42:1-2

irst, let me urge you to remember that what is important is where your heart is —not your mind or tongue as much as your heart—for *"out of the abundance of the heart the mouth speaks"* (Matthew 12:34). The Word reminds us we need to guard our hearts with all diligence, *"for out of it spring the issues of life"* (Proverbs 4:23). In seeking the Lord in prayer, let our quest be from the heart and the spirit, not in empty superficialities.

First Prayer Concerns

We'll ultimately learn that what we say to the Lord is not nearly so important as what He says to us. We'll ultimately learn that what is on our lips is much less important than what is in our hearts. But most of us think the only way to communicate with God is with words.

As God works in our hearts a new desire to seek Him, we may find among our prayers: "Lord, let me know my need of You." "Lord, give me a holy hunger for Yourself." "Lord, teach me how to worship you in spirit and in truth." "Lord, may Your name be praised."

Don't let it bother you if you haven't any feeling for such prayers at first. If you don't seem able to mean them, tell Him so. Ask Him to begin making it possible for you to mean them. If you feel hypocritical in praying what you don't feel, just pray what's really on your heart. Tell Him what you do think and feel. Just be honest with Him. He knows, cares, and understands. When you're honest with Him, He can begin the necessary work in your heart.

Now, there are some things you mustn't do. Don't be content with praying selfish, self-centered prayers. Don't ignore His call on your affections. Don't pretend you're responding when in your heart you aren't—you're just going through the motions. Be real with God, even if it's only to tell Him you can't do it. He'll have to do it, if it's to be done.

Prayer Journals

Try writing down your thoughts, prayers, concerns, and responses to God in a prayer journal. Be absolutely honest with the Lord in everything you write. You may be amazed at how much it helps.

You may find keeping a prayer list to be a great help in intercessory prayer. However, when you can't pray for each person or situation as thoroughly as you would like, commit them all to the Lord to exercise His loving care over them. To focus your concern, lay your hand on the pages as you give them to God.

You may also find keeping a devotional diary to be of help and encouragement to yourself and perhaps even to others. Simply write down your prayer thoughts to God.

Another encouraging aid is to record answers to prayer, the loved ones who have met the Lord as you prayed for them, the financial blessings that arrived just as you needed them, the healings of body and spirit, and even when God denied your requests to bring about His better plans. Consulting this section when you seem to be in a dry season will remind you that God is lovingly in control.

Ways of Communing with Him

I don't want to tell you how to approach the Lord. Yet I don't want, either, to fail to give you what help I can. So let me merely make this broad range of suggestions and trust His Spirit to be your personal tutor. In seeking to give Him your loving attention in devotional prayer, you may do any or all of the following as He may lead.

Converse with Him as friend with friend. Share your most private concerns, your failures and frustrations, your sense of guilt and need.

Listen. Just give Him an attentive ear, and let Him do with it as He will. Recognize your utter dependence on Him, His mercy and grace.

Tell Him you want and need Him. Seek after Him. Give expression to the longing for Him placed within by the Holy Spirit. Long for Him regardless of the results. Desire Him in all the ways your seeking heart will devise.

Seek to agree with Him in everything. Seek not to fear His plans and purposes for you, but to let Him teach you to trust Him.

Joy and rejoice in Him and His love. Sing hymns of worship, praise, or thanksgiving.

Ways of Seeking Him

Think on Him. Meditate on Him, His person, His character, and His work as Creator, Sustainer, Redeemer, and Eternal King. Contemplate His infinite perfection.

Thank Him that He is all-powerful, all-knowing, always present, infinite and eternal, unchanging, surpassing finite comprehension. Thank Him that He is love, that He is faithful and kind, gracious and merciful, true and pure, righteous and holy, just and good.

Rejoice that He is worthy of love, worship, adoration, and praise. Praise Him that He is made unto us wisdom, righteousness, sanctification, and redemption. Praise Him that He is the way, the truth, and the life. Give Him glory that He is the bread, water, and word of life, and that He has become our salvation, light, shepherd, resurrection, strength, and shield. Give Him honor that He is the God of peace and hope. Praise Him that He is the ultimate satisfaction for all we ever long for or need.

Worship and adore Him. Offer Him back the love He first gives you. Thank and praise Him for all His goodness, yes, but much more for Himself. Joy and rejoice in Him. See Him in His love, compassion, mercy, and grace to us. Rejoice in His entire trustworthiness.

Ways to Long for Him

Long to be filled with Him and His Spirit for no selfish purpose, only for His own pleasure and glory. Long that He might be praised and honored, glorified and magnified, worshiped and adored. Yearn to please Him and give Him pleasure.

Long that you may be purified from everything that does not magnify Him and bring praise, glory, and honor to Him. Long that He show you your loathsome sin-sickness, your depravity and degradation. Long that He show you your need of Him with His love, grace, mercy, forgiveness, cleansing, and peace.

Praying in a Meek and Quiet Spirit

You may find yourself moving slowly from a lot of activity to more quietness and receptivity of spirit before Him. (See Psalm 62:5, 130:5, and 131:2.) You may learn to come nearer the end of your independent activity to rest quietly and trustfully in Him. Have no other purpose than to be with Him, assured that He will do whatever pleases Him in and for you.

Let Him bring all resistance to an end. He doesn't have to prove Himself to you, speak to you, or instruct you. Rest in quietness before Him, knowing that He is doing His will in you and on your behalf, whether you feel it or not.

Thoughts come and go without greatly impinging on the meek and quiet spirit that may return as readily to its rest in the Lord as a bird to its accustomed perch. Each thought that is of any consequence may be committed unobtrusively to the Lord in passing, as the meek and quiet spirit continues its rest in Him.

When that meek and quiet spirit is moved to express its love of the Lord or to worship, thank, or praise Him, it may do so without strain, urgency, or disturbance of your peace and rest in Him. What a joy and delight. But be careful not to make much of the joy, or even of this time of special quietness with Him. Magnify the Lord only for Himself!

An Example

Let me outline for you one way the time of devotional prayer may be profitably spent. The following suggestions are offered as guidelines for those who need a model, not as a rigid structure to be strictly adhered to. Prayer times vary as the Lord gives fresh direction.

Read a portion of Scripture, good daily devotional, or part of a helpful book.

If there's anything on your heart to talk to the Lord about, share it with Him, especially anything that has put a barrier between you and Him. Write it all down if possible. Be as absolutely open and honest as you can. Don't go looking for anything. Just share with the Lord whatever is on your heart. Confess any known sin to the Lord. If any dispute exists between you and another person, commit yourself unhesitatingly to make it right.

Commit all of it into the Lord's keeping, trusting Him to do all that needs to be done about each facet. Don't make more of any of it than God makes, but respond fully to His speaking.

When you're done, or if there is nothing you want to share with the Lord, open a good topical Bible. Select a subject heading such as God, Jesus Christ, one of His attributes or names, prayer, praise, worship, love, or trust. Or, choose a passage of Scripture such as Isaiah 6, Revelation 4 and 5, Ezekiel 1, Job 40-42, or a worship Psalm.

Read for a few moments, soaking in the Scriptures. Let the Lord draw you to Himself. Seek as much as possible to be occupied with Him alone. Remain for a time in loving, submissive prayer communion with Him.

When your mind wanders and you sense the need of further assistance for your prayer communion, let your eyes fall again to the open page before you. Let them fall there, not so much to learn anything in particular as to allow the Spirit to warm your heart again to the Lord Himself. When He has, return to quiet prayer communion with Him.

Whether He moves you to energetically seek Him, adoringly worship Him, or quietly wait on Him, do it. Repeat this as often as you find it helpful.

As you rest contentedly before Him in a meek and quiet spirit, you will find yourself relinquishing all to Him without exerting effort. Sometimes He will just relieve you of the no-longer-wanted burden of your selfish desires.

Practical Guidance

Don't try to feel or sense, picture or envision the Lord much. God the Father and the Spirit are incorporeal, without bodies. He reveals His character to us in His Word. He is whatever we need. That must be sufficient.

To think of Jesus in the flesh is of limited help. Paul determined to know Him no longer after the flesh (2 Corinthians 5:16). Nonetheless, meditating on His perfect life, sacrifice, and resurrection or to recall Him seated in His divine humanity at the right hand of God in power is not amiss, should you find it beneficial. Just so it doesn't hinder you in remembering that He is in you in power, and you are in Him resting content in His working. Let Him reveal Himself to you as He will.

If the effort to wait quietly before Him is at any time more a liability than an asset in your search for the Lord in love, talk to Him about Himself. Talk to Him about who He is, and your relationship with Him—or about anything else, as He may lead.

Remember you are engaged in devotional prayer. Your attention is to be directed to Him and His things, not to you and yours. Anything that long robs you of His peace can't be of Him.

As you seek Him, the responsibilities of the day may interject themselves into your mind as distractions. To dispose of them, you may pause a moment to put them on a list of things to do. However, limit this practice so it doesn't usurp your time and interest. Rather than relieving you of the cares of this life, it can direct your attention from the Lord to them.

Returning to Rest

Rest in the LORD, and wait patiently for Him;
...Cease from anger, and forsake wrath;
*   do not fret—it only causes harm.*
...Those who wait upon the LORD,
*   they shall inherit the earth.*
But the meek shall inherit the earth,
*   and shall delight themselves*
*   in the abundance of peace.*
*   —Psalm 37:7-9, 11*

We may find ourselves disappointed that returning to sweet fellowship with the Lord can be difficult. We may have been drawn away from the intimacy of our communion with Him since last we met alone. We may be beset with matters that are comparatively unimportant in the light of eternity. We could have become mentally and emotionally reentangled with the things of this life, things we'd left in God's able hands when last we met together. Our attitudes may even have reverted from rest to rush, from peace to push, from confidence in

God to mistrust of Him, from harmony and unity with the Lord to rebellion, resistance, and resentment.

Alone with Him again, we start over to look to Him. We begin again to see Him in His infinite perfection, His entire trustworthiness, His love, compassion, mercy, and grace.

We may be surprised at how long it takes to find Him attractive once more. It may take quite a while for our attention to be drawn away from ourselves, our problems, needs, and wishes to Him in loving worship. This distraction from Him produces the need for us to spend so long alone with Him. Start stretching your time with Him from wherever it is now to something more adequate.

Hopefully, as the Lord continues to draw us and we keep responding, we will walk more closely with Him throughout the day. Then we will spend less devotional time relinquishing our resistance and returning to His arms.

More Practical Guidance

In your devotional prayer, fears should subside in trust in the trustworthy God. All your concerns are to be rested quietly in His tender care. Fleshly rebellion, resentments, and resistance are to be replaced with loving surrender to your loving Lord. Sin of any kind ought to become distasteful, freely repented of, and gladly forsaken. Your heart should be prepared willingly to confess any sin to any person sinned against, as well as to the Lord.

Peace should replace anxiety. Gentleness, love, and sensitivity must displace anger, hatred, and bitterness. Meekness and humility must succeed pride and arrogance. Dependence on almighty God needs to supersede your spirit of independence. Quietness and rest of spirit should replace the constant pressure to do something. Praise and thanksgiving to the Lord must dissolve your complaining spirit. His life becomes the source of your life, replacing your independent self-life.

Now, achieving all of this may seem like a lot of hard work. I'm afraid that's what many of us make of it, without much success. An easier way is that of the meek and quiet spirit. At first it may not seem to be available to you, but as you continue to seek the Lord in prayer, He'll surely bring you to the place where He can give you at least something of that meek and quiet spirit. You will find Him silently replacing your selfish desires with His, your very self-centeredness with Himself.

In everything your purpose is to yield to the Lord your worshipful, trusting, and receptive attention in loving submission and quiet meekness of spirit. Out of this every good thing He has for you will ultimately come.

CHAPTER 10

The Prayer of Love

*True worshipers will worship the Father
in spirit and truth:
for the Father is seeking such to worship Him.
God is Spirit,
and those who worship Him
must worship Him in spirit and truth.*
—John 4:23-24

*Seek first the kingdom [realm] of God
and His righteousness,
and all these things shall be added to you.*
—Matthew 6:33

*In everything give thanks,
for this is the will of God
in Christ Jesus for you.*
—1 Thessalonians 5:18

What is the purpose of devotional prayer? Surely one of God's purposes in prayer is to bring us to a place of closer harmony with Him and of growing dependence on Him. As we let God be God and learn to respond to Him as such, our differences dissolve and our independence subsides.

To come to Him, yielding Him our loving, responsive attention is to allow Him to transform us little by little into more of His likeness. Partly a purging process, this relieves us of our burden of sin, pride, rebellion, resistance, and resentment. Given the awesome reality of our awful depravity (Jeremiah 17:9), it is hard to imagine any Christian belittling the necessity of this spiritual exercise.

Worshipful Prayer

Come to Him worshipfully then, seeking only Him. Be relieved of your concern for things of time and space to commune lovingly with Him in the dimension of the Spirit.

To keep our attention on things temporal and physical rather than on God and things eternal and spiritual is to incapacitate our spirits from worshiping Him in the realm of the Spirit. So the elemental aim of private communion with God is freedom from earthly entanglements to worship Him in love.

Our calling is to love and worship God, now and through all eternity. But worship is far more, and perhaps other, than we have thought. We may worship Him with words, thoughts, or hymns, but our hearts may worship the Lord without words. We may worship Him with the loving attention of a quiet, waiting spirit. Words may lie, but not the tender and meek spirit. So may we worship Him by simply enjoying gratefully who He is. We may just soak up His love, or even Himself, and that may be worship. We may let go of all that has displaced Him in our thoughts or affections, and that, too, may be a genuine act of worship. But there's more even than these.

Sacrifice of Self

At the end of the eleventh chapter of Romans, Paul sings a doxology of praise to God as the transition from the doctrinal discussion to the practical application section which begins in chapter twelve. There he calls on us to perform a sensible service: offering ourselves once-for-all as a perpetual sacrifice on the altar of love to God. That is worship!

To be reconfirming this in continual self-sacrifice would surely be worship delighting His Father heart even more. Are you prepared, on leaving your quiet time, to be a living sacrifice? Are you willing to die daily to your desires that He may accomplish His pleasure in you? No less an objective should be ours.

We can start toward this goal by coming to God in devotional prayer, with a meek and quiet spirit, needing Him, being still before Him. Yield your concerns for earthly things to

Him. Give Him your attention as fully as possible. As He enables, all the ungodly selves of self-reliance, self-dependence, self-pride, self-will, self-effort, and self-love along with rebellion, resistance, and resentment will dissolve to be replaced by the all-encompassing God.

As He becomes the focus of your loving, worshipful attention, let Him relieve you increasingly of your fear, anxiety, worry, and tension. Release them to Him in quiet trust, confidence, and love. Let go of everything into His control. Refuse to hold onto anything, to seek to control anything, or to be controlled by anything but God Himself.

Sometimes, you will release them one by one as each raises its ugly head. More often, you may simply rest content in Him, letting go of everything in general to Him, to find your temporal interests, fears, and concerns dissolving in His loving presence. Nothing needs to be of undue concern to you because all is of such intimate concern to the Almighty. Be assured He is in the business of perfectly taking care of all your cares.

In devotional prayer, be willing to let go of all that is on your heart and mind that pre-empts His position there. Give it all to Him. If you don't, there will be no room for Him, and you will come into your prayer closet and leave again in frustration.

Let God Guide

Beware of focusing on anything other than the Lord Himself, the one reality to which we need to gravitate in utter dependency. Let it be in rest and peace rather than in our independent self-efforts. He works as we wait in quiet confidence, not as we struggle and strive, even to give Him our loving attention.

Beware of seeking to know Him with your intellect. Only your spirit is really equipped to know Him. So come to Him with as sensitive a spirit as He'll enable, even more than with a willing mind.

Our Experiences Will Differ

You may be disappointed that sometimes you can't find the same sweet communion with Him that you do at other times. Don't be unduly concerned when nothing seems to happen in your time with Him. You may feel barren, dull, empty, and hopeless.

The real danger is that you may turn from seeking the Lord to self-pity. You may even accuse God of not rewarding you for your faithfulness. If you do, may God enable you to recognize with horror the rebellion such responses reveal and run again into His arms of love. Realize that He is graciously teaching you to walk by faith and not by sight.

On the other hand, some of our experiences may be surpassingly glorious. We may have the joy of coming to rest in silent awe, content to be lost in Him and His love, nobody apart from Him, the struggle gone, the fears subsided, the needs met in Him. Words may be inconsequential, thoughts inadequate. To those who, at such a time, feel themselves immersed in God, the experience is sacred and indescribable.

Lost in His Love

The nature, duration, and intensity of such experiences may vary greatly. But for that moment even more than other occasions, we may find: all our desire is for Him; we trust Him implicitly; He is our joy and rejoicing; He alone is our hope; our hearts are gentle, tender, and pliable to Him; we relinquish everything to Him, seeking to retain nothing for ourselves; nothing He could ask of us is too great; we are gladly weak that He in us might be strong; no earthly possession is, at that moment, worth seeking after or holding onto; we could not possibly wish to disobey our lovely Lord; the thought that we could displease Him is more than we can bear; our greatest pleasure is to please Him and give Him pleasure.

If we think of ourselves at all, we despise our sins, our sinfulness, and our selfishness. Our innate depravity is a horrid burden we would be rid of. We are pained by anything other than Him. We would gladly die for Him. Our dearest desire is to be swallowed up in His infinite love, lost in Him. We yearn to be with Him where He is; yet, we're quietly at rest before Him, content with whatever He allows. Our focus is removed from ourselves and our spiritual growth to center on Him alone.

Not Experiences, But Our God

Any or all of these responses, and others, may be ours in more or less intensity. We may experience something whenever God gives us the meek and quiet spirit that waits restfully before Him. While we dare not seek the experience, we may seek to be at home in Him as often as we will. We'll always profit, if we don't come looking for some selfish benefit or feeling, and then accuse God of letting us down because we didn't get it.

Whatever experiences are ours, we must be sure to make little of them, much of Him. Don't, my dear one, let any experience replace our glorious Lord in your affections.

If He permits you to have special feelings or experiences, receive what He gives. If He refrains from giving them, be grateful that He knows best. If He deprives you of that which He once gave, turn to Him for His enabling grace to trust His love expressed even in such a way. Continue unabatedly to seek Him only.

Quiet Time

In your quiet time, be as alone with God as you can possibly be. Seek to give Him pleasure. Rest in Him, His love, and His peace. Yield everything to Him so He can be God to you, communicating Himself and any of His gifts that He can safely give, taking away what separates and grieves.

When we come in devotional prayer to look to the Lord in worship, we must first have our hearts and minds relieved of the burden of self-centeredness. Consciously or unconsciously, this must take place before we can give Him our loving, worshipful attention. Our needs, problems, wants, hopes, and things, all need to be displaced and replaced by Him. Until we trust ourselves and all our interests to Him in implicit confidence, are we not in bondage to our independent selves that makes genuinely worshiping Him impossible?

In our devotional praying, even though we may be taken up with concern for the spiritual rather than the temporal, we may become consumed, not with God, but merely with our relationship with Him. This may degenerate into simply preoccupation with our feelings. As a result, we continue in our self-centeredness rather than being delivered from it into the God-centeredness we seek.

The Prayer of Silence

If you come across an expression such as this in your reading, I suggest you see it as a quietness of heart, mind, and spirit that reflects the peace of God, in contrast to the cerebral approach of thinking or reasoning, the emotional approach of anxious concern, or the supposedly spiritual approach of feelings of God's presence and work. The importance of words and concrete thoughts is subjected to that of a spirit quietly waiting on God.

However, I urge you not to be deluded into trying to sit by the hour before God trying to do and think nothing. All my attempts have accomplished is to put me quickly to sleep.

Value that inward peace and silence that listens to God. See what militates against it, and seek to see them reduced: hurry, worry, flurry; negative responses—finding anything in our circumstances unacceptable. God must change us on the inside so we can grow toward accepting everything as from Him.

A Deep Yearning

We may find ourselves longing whole-heartedly after the Lord. We may find ourselves crying out for Him, wanting Him to reveal Himself to us, needing Him, yearning for Him until our hearts are near breaking.

Then, as we learn the value of resting quietly at peace in Him, we may abandon this zealous seeking for the Lord. We may even conclude that it is of the flesh and needs to be forsaken as though it were an anxious care. However, this active seeking and longing after the Lord may be the open door to resting in Him when all else fails. So let your heart be Spirit-led to long for the Lord as He wills.

You may also find yourself reluctant to tell the Lord how much you love Him when you see how shallow and selfish your love really is, how little gratitude and self-sacrifice there is in it. Don't pretend it is any more than it is. Just be grateful that in His love He has given self-centered, self-serving you any selfless love at all. Thank Him that Christ in you loves fully and freely where the old you cannot. Thank Him that He in you meets His Father's desires where you can't. Praise and give Him glory that you are complete in Him in all respects, including these where you feel so unworthy.

A Gentled Spirit

One who learned to commune and walk with God many years ago said the first thing

104

he noticed as a response to God's working was a gentling of his spirit. While I have a very long way yet to go in this regard, I can add my testimony to his. We need to see gentleness as the Spirit-induced virtue it is.

In the life in the Spirit there's no room for harshness and unkindness. Of course, there may be those who inappropriately apply these labels to unbending firmness on behalf of righteousness, but we must make no excuse for any hardness of heart or harshness of manner. Remember that others may most readily see the Lord in us in our meek and gentle spirit.

Praise and Thanksgiving

Rejoice in the LORD always.
Again I will say, rejoice!
Let your gentleness be known to all men.
The LORD is at hand.
Be anxious for nothing, but in everything by
prayer and supplication, with thanksgiving,
let your requests be made known to God;
and the peace of God,
which surpasss all understanding, will guard
your hearts and minds through Christ Jesus.
Finally, brethren, whatever things are true,
whatever things are noble,
whatever things are just,
whatever things are pure,
whatever things are lovely,

whatever things are of good report,
if there is any virtue and
if there is anything praiseworthy—
meditate on these things.
—Philippians 4:4-8

Have you ever noticed how Paul, in urging God's people to pray, repeatedly asked them to pray without anxiety but with rejoicing, praise, and thanksgiving; and how he repeatedly cited peace as the result of thanksgiving? You may be surprised to learn that heartfelt thanksgiving may be the most important aspect of the Christian life. To a large extent, whether you live in thanksgiving or not determines what happens to your spiritual life and your relationship with the Lord.

A thankful spirit is the peak of positive response to the realization that God is working all things together for our good. Complaining, bitterness, anger, anxiety, frustration, hatred, strife, push, shove, hurry, and worry are all the opposite of thankfulness. They show that we really don't believe God is always working everything together for our good.

Never Defend Negative Responses

Positive, thankful, trusting, non-resistant, unperturbed responses to our circumstances must replace the old negative ones if we're going to respond positively and lovingly to God and His work in our lives. Seek never to let yourself cover up the defiling character of complaining, grumbling, thanklessness, discontent, and resentment. When you do, let Him teach you to be quick to acknowledge and turn from it. In all likelihood, you can't yet praise your wonderful Lord and give Him thanks for allowing the difficulties in your life to be the means of bringing you blessing and benefit, but you will as He enables.

Continual Communion

Pray without ceasing.
—1 Thessalonians 5:17

Devotion and communion aren't just for prayer time. We should seek to be in constant quiet communion and communication with the Lord. Seek to fellowship with the Lord out of love, free from pressure. Let Him teach you to discuss everything with Him as with a best friend. Talk to Him rather than yourself.

It won't do that we stop worshiping when we leave the quiet place! Always an act of worship for us is simply to rest in the reality that Christ in us is all-sufficient for our needs all the day every moment. So it is that we rest, content in Him and His working on our behalf.

If we long for God to reveal Himself to us, it must be in order that He may reveal Himself in us. So may He be attractive in us to others in whom He may reveal Himself, and in them to still others, and so on. Anything less is selfishness, and has no place in our worship.

As we continue to look to Him, human self-interest will be swallowed up in His interests. Self-pleasing gives way little by little to our longing to please Him, to give Him pleasure. We long to see His majestic perfection be made known and His name be praised.

May the Lord become our center. Let Him be precious. Stand in awe of Him, yet accept His Father love. Prayer must not be what we want, but what He wants; not what or who we are, but what and who He is; not our love but His; not our importance, but His.

CHAPTER 11

Dimensions of True Prayer

*Do not seek what you should eat
or what you should drink.
...For all these things
the nations of the world seek after,
and your Father knows
that you need these things.
But seek the kingdom of God,
and all these things shall be added to you.
Do not fear, little flock,
for it is your Father's good pleasure
to give you the kingdom.
...For where your treasure is,
there your heart will be also.
—Luke 12:29-34*

Have I seemed to imply that all our prayer time will be consumed with giving the Lord and matters eternal and spiritual all our attention? Perhaps it seems that way. As we learn to seek Him, a much larger proportion of longer prayer periods than we ever previously dreamed will be devoted to Him alone.

When we've let go of everything into His care, praised and worshiped Him only, and rested ourselves in Him, at that moment to ask anything for ourselves may be offensive to our spirits. But, of course, the time spent apart with the Lord includes more than the prayer of devotion or communion.

We have seen that devotional prayer itself may contain, in addition to the seeking of God for Himself alone, instruction and correction, repentance and confession. To be complete, prayer will also include what many have surmised composed all of it: intercession, petition, and prayerful Bible study.

The Role of Intercession

You will make your prayer to Him,
He will hear you,
And you will pay your vows.
You will declare a thing,
And it will be established for you;
So light will shine on your ways.
When they cast you down, and you say,
"Exaltation will come!"
Then He will save the humble person.
He will even deliver one who is not innocent.
Yes, he will be delivered
by the purity of your hands.
—Job 22:27-30

Our emphasis has been on devotional prayer—seeking the Lord for Himself alone. In this way He may become to us all He longs to be—the very center and circumference of our lives. As He fills us, He then simply overflows into the lives of others. Joy replaces the awful stifling compulsion that characterizes so many Christians' lives.

But the heart tender to the Lord simply can't avoid ejaculatory prayers of both petition for personal needs and intercession. Even if you wanted to, you couldn't resist the urge! If you fail to spend time in prayer for the needs of others, you'll certainly find the Holy Spirit reminding you of this responsibility.

You may have felt petition and intercession have been neglected in this book, and I want to see they have their proper place in your heart. Father God wants you to come to Him with all your personal needs and cares. In times of intercession, you may discover as much blessing for yourself as for those for whom you pray. As God gives you a genuine, heart concern for others, you may find great release in your own spirit to respond to His Spirit.

However, if you're not ready for a serious ministry of intercession, there's no need to put yourself under bondage. Simply commit it to the Lord to open this door to you in His own way and time. Intercession may become one of the great joys and privileges of your life.

What about Petition?

If you abide in Me,
and My words abide in you,
you will ask what you desire,
and it shall be done for you.
—John 15:7

How can God make such a promise? When your heart is submitted happily to the Lord and His pleasure, your will matches His.

But be careful. Our deceitful willfulness and self-pleasing knows no bounds. The danger in prayers of petition is, first, that they tend often to reflect our selfishness and lack of submission to the Lord, His interests, and His will. Second, they often are accompanied by anxious worry. We've already characterized worry as the sin of mistrust.

When our supplicatory prayers are submitted to His will, we'll often recognize that we don't know what He wants in a given situation. We'll pray simply that He'll do all that will glorify His name, or that He will do better for the person for whom we're concerned than we could ask or think.

Nonetheless, we need to believe God honors specific prayers for specific needs and surely answers every prayer prayed in His will. We need to live in constant restful anticipation of His intervening on behalf of His trusting children and those they entrust to His care.

I get a lot of satisfaction out of just committing people or circumstances into His care, and leaving them there for Him to do with exactly as will best please and praise Him. I don't see the purpose of asking God to do things I'm not confident He wants to do. So I'd rather give the person or matter into His capable hands and caring heart.

Today I talked to the Lord about a lady I've mentioned whom I hadn't heard from for a while. I was concerned and wanted to hear from her again. I did. The day before yesterday the same thing happened with someone else. Yes, the Lord cares about even our smallest concerns. The problem is that especially in what we see as big concerns our self-will shows up and inhibits God's response.

The issue is not nearly so much the words of prayer but the heart of trust. Let us trust Him always *to do exceedingly abundantly above all that we ask or think* (Ephesians 3:20), that He may receive eternal praise.

A Heart in Tune with God

When our hearts are being attuned to the Lord, we naturally share more and more of what comes our way with Him whether in words or in spirit. When we're attuned with

Him, we'll want to be sure that what we want is what He wants, whether for ourselves or others.

Having established that we want what He wants—or are allowing Him to change us so we do—then we can confidently expect that what we both want is what He'll give us.

It's abominable how we've abused the statements of our Lord that He'll give us whatever we ask in His name. James 4:3 clearly states that we mustn't expect to get what we ask for selfishly: *"You ask and do not receive, because you ask amiss, that you may spend it on your pleasures."* We should always have realized, even without this passage, that to ask in His name is to ask on His authority, His power of attorney, as it were. He obviously can't and won't give us such authority unless we're asking for what He wants us to have.

So our chief concern in prayers of petition and intercession should be to accept what God wants without concern for what we want. Only then can we claim His prayer promises. As we come closer to the heart of God, we'll find petitions for ourselves and intercession for others becoming more a spontaneous reaching out for the will of God to be done. This will displace the former pleading with Him to conform to our wishes. We'll find ourselves increasingly abandoning our desires, purposes, goals, and ambitions for His. Prayer will become more nearly the beating of our hearts in tune with the heart of God.

The Place of the Written Word

We know nothing for sure about God or things eternal or spiritual apart from the divine revelation of His Word. We have no other basis for our prayer life than the written Word. We know the character of the God with whom we have relationship only by His Word.

Right here, some who would seek the Lord are stymied. They never take time to learn what the Word reveals about the character of God, foolishly holding onto their own twisted concepts of what God is like. If we are to learn to walk with God in a Christianity that really works, we need to give a priority place to finding Him as He is in His Word.

We need to know and understand what God is really like, to see Him revealed in all His beauty and attractiveness to the blood-bought soul. Feed your heart and thoughts by reading carefully the biblical revelation of the Lord and its call to worship Him. Let Him teach you who He really is in His infinite perfection, how He works, and what His will is. Get a good topical Bible and read the passages about God, Jesus Christ, and the Holy Spirit.

You may find encouragement from literature that genuinely points you to the Lord.

However, don't get so wrapped up in what others have to say that you miss the voice of the Lord speaking through His Scriptures.

Let the Word Be Your Guide

Occasionally in your time of devotional prayer, you may feel that God has revealed something special to you. As great as this is, it may feed your pride and encourage your spirit of independence from the Lord. You may even be misled.

Keep your Bible, concordance, and other helps for Bible study handy. Whenever you feel that the Lord has taught you something, however delightfully new, submit it to the Lord, and verify it from His Word. If you can't verify it from the entirety of the Word of God, lay it aside until you can. To proceed without that confirmation is dangerous in the extreme and never permissible.

Further, the confirmation must be genuine. To impose your revelation on Scripture and try to make Scripture say what you want it to say is wrong and can lead you into being deluded and others being deceived.

Submit everything to the written Word. Never proceed against its direction.

CHAPTER 12

Overcoming Hindrances to Prayer

*Oh, that I knew where I might find Him,
that I might come to His seat!
...Look, I go forward, but He is not there,
and backward, but I cannot perceive Him.*
—*Job 23:3, 8*

Sometimes even the most sincere seekers feel as if their prayers aren't reaching beyond the ceiling. Sometimes in spite of your best attempts to practice what you've learned, all seems to end in frustration. Sometimes you can't worship God, seek Him, love Him, praise Him, thank Him, or wait on Him in rest and peace. The ability to relinquish everything to Him in loving surrender has just disappeared!

Accepting these dry times as from the Lord without anger or resentment is to trust Him to bring good from all He allows in the prayer time as elsewhere. Still, the fact is that this is a frustrating experience. If long continued and not responded to wisely, this may become spiritually debilitating, even leading to some abandoning the quest for more of God. To those discouraged seekers, I offer some practical suggestions and guidelines for dealing with times when you seem to have hit a brick wall.

Removing the Blockages

Unaware of our neediness and sin, we may have been living in practical independence from the Lord. So when we come to Him in prayer, He is not in all our thoughts. Some sin or disobedience may be unconfessed and unforsaken. This will not do. Agree with God immediately. Confess and forsake it gladly for His sake. Let nothing deter you!

We may be distracted from the Lord by the things of this life. Paul desired *"that you may serve the LORD without distraction"* (1 Corinthians 7:35). We may have replaced our attention to Him with attention to TV, radio, or idle talk. We may not have taken time and opportunity to turn our attention and affection back to Him often throughout the day. As a result, we may find our attention firmly fixed on things rather than on the Lord.

Just being in a hurry can get us so wound up that we have little time, or thought, or room for God, or even for others.

We may secretly resent some circumstance God permits in our life or some demand we fear He may be making of us. We may be resenting Him for not giving us what we seek in prayer.

Our negative reactions of resentment, anger, bitterness, fear, anxiety, and a harsh, unkind spirit may have replaced our trust and rest in the Lord and the gentle tenderness of spirit He brings. It really isn't hard to see why a gulf separates us and the Lord. That chasm is bridged by releasing to Him and His mastery all that separates or offends, and then returning to Him to rest contentedly.

We may not be spending enough time with the Lord to allow the Holy Spirit to break down all our resistances and remove our attention from earthly things to Himself. The whole of devotional prayer is to be centered on God.

We may be guilty of wanting more from this time than Him alone. If we don't let the Lord bring us to the place of being content with Him alone, what else can we be but discontent?

We may not have become willing to relinquish everything to Him, let go of our desire to control things, and be restfully assured He's safely in charge of everything.

We may be trying rather than trusting. The longer we remain with our attention as much as possible quietly directed toward Him in whatever way He makes possible, the freer we may be to receive from Him whatever He wishes to communicate to us. We can't prescribe to Him the nature of our relationship.

Dealing with Drowsiness

As you're alone with the Lord, occasionally you may fall into a sleep in which God is still your center and focus. This you need not resist, provided you benefit spiritually, not merely physically from it. Sometimes it has seemed to help my struggling heart come to a place of rest in Him.

However, if there is no spiritual benefit from it, you may need to move around, walk, or speak aloud in order to stay awake. Take a break for strenuous physical exercise. Deep breathing might work, as well as opening a window for some fresh air. I've occasionally given myself a good hard slap on the face. Sometimes I've thanked the Lord for the interruption of my wife, daughter, grand-daughter, or the phone to waken me or keep me awake.

Try writing down your thoughts. Be careful that you aim at simplicity, candor, and honesty rather than a pretty spiritual diary. God may use it for much more than keeping you awake.

Use your Bible and devotional aids, but you may find more help in interrupting your devotional prayers to intercede for others.

If falling asleep becomes a perpetual problem, go to bed earlier, much earlier if necessary. Usually it is the evening hours that we waste anyway.

A Wandering Mind

Most of us will experience difficulties with a short attention span or lack of concentration during prayer times on occasion. First of all, do not fret or stew about it. To worry is to mistrust God. To mistrust Him is one of the most abominable of sins.

If you focus on the wandering, you're certainly not focusing on the Lord. Just be quietly at home in Him. Trust Him. Allow Him to draw your affections back to Him as He will.

You may find keeping your Bible or a devotional book open in front of you and referring to it often helps with this problem, too. Special passages that revere the Lord, for instance in the Psalms, can easily turn your focus back to Him.

You may also find help from meditating on the characteristics of God. Find Him worthy of all honor, worship, praise, and adoration.

Writing down your prayer thoughts may help limit the wandering mind problem. So may periods of loving intercession for others.

Enemies of Rest

Some enemies of rest in the Lord are: lack of trust in Him, fear, uncertainty, impatience, worry, anxiety, contentiousness, excessive concern for opinions of others, self-imposed or self-met deadlines, resentment, bitterness, anger, envy, jealousy, lust, possessiveness, pretense, fantasy, unreality, selfishness, covetousness, self-righteousness, pride, independence from God, rebellion, willful disobedience. In other words, sins that separate from God prevent resting in Him.

The presence of any of these, when recognized, should set off warning bells that ring, "Give it to Jesus. Give it to Jesus." To walk without harboring or defending them, releasing them to Jesus as they're recognized, is to walk in the light, relaxing in the joy of the Lord.

We have no reason for tension to rule our lives. If we are weak enough, meek enough, willing enough to be needy, we can always, upon recognizing the cause, relinquish it to Him. The tranquility of resting content in Him can replace the tensions. Waves of rest will return after each resurgence of tension as we live in continuing preference for God and His order of peace rather than for ourselves and our order of constant restlessness. This relinquishing and relaxing can lead to the beautiful release of rest, peace, joy, and liberty in the Lord that we may have only dreamed about.

Stuck on a Treadmill

Why do we make so little progress in prayer and our relationships with the Lord? We simply must die to having any hope in ourselves so it may all be in Him alone.

We had the sentence of death in ourselves,
that we should not trust in ourselves
but in God who raises the dead.
—2 Corinthians 1:9

Always carrying about in the body
the dying of the LORD Jesus,
that the life of Jesus also
may be manifested in our body.
For we who live are always delivered
to death for Jesus' sake,
that the life of Jesus also
may be manifested in our mortal flesh.
—2 Corinthians 4:10-11

This is why the life that is in Christ is repugnant to many Christians and neglected by many teachers. Die they will not. While initially attractive because of all the promise it holds, when the Christ-life demands our death, all that is of the old man rises up in rebellion.

God offers us Himself and every good thing. But the best, kindest, loveliest, most wonderful gift He offers is our death stroke. To this we say no, and ultimately to all He offers. He can live fully and freely only in those who have willingly accepted the slaying of their independent selves.

We may not be willing to come to Him to be emptied of ourselves, to die to our independent selves. Trying to worship Him, love Him, thank Him, give Him our attention and affection is useless apart from recognizing our sin and neediness, and repudiating ourselves for Him. But we need to be sure we look only long enough at ourselves to see our ugly sin and failure, and then to run back quickly to Father.

We have nothing to give God—not even loving attention. Our focus is naturally consumed on ourselves. We're not natively loving. In fact, our attempt to give Him our attention—to love Him, worship Him, or give Him pleasure—may benefit us most by showing us we cannot do anything that is good. If it is good, He alone is its author and empowerer.

So, give up on yourself. Release everything into His tender care. If you can do nothing more, you can seek to rest content in Him.

God sometimes seems to withdraw Himself for His own good purposes. We must accept this also as a gift of His love and remain as faithful in our times with Him as though it weren't so. Often when we feel nothing is transpiring between us and the Lord, a great deal is really happening. In our blindness and ignorance, we simply are not able to see it.

Whatever the Lord sends you in your time with Him, submit yourself to Him and to it. Let Him be Lord of the quiet time, too. Especially be sure it isn't just feelings you are missing. God hasn't promised you feelings, but Himself. Trust Him to keep His word. Be satisfied that He is there with you, that you are in Him and He in you. Rest and be content.

Be Sure You Have a Solid Foundation

Christ is in you; you are in Him. When these become more than mere words to your spirit, this wonderful reality can lay a foundation for everything else you learn about your relationship with the Lord. Christ is in you, your hope of glory, as stated in Colossians 1:27.

And you are complete in Him,
who is the head of all principality and power.
—Colossians 2:10

Christ is your life (see Colossians 3:4), your all-sufficiency. You are at home in Him where you may rest quietly in the glad assurance that He will supply all you need. For your prayer time this means that, whatever happens in it, you can be at home in Him. You can be content that He is doing and being everything you need then and there whether you feel like it or not.

To begin with then, as you look for a cure for the frustration you feel at having those difficult prayer periods, you must depend on the reliability of the written Word, not on feelings of any sort. He is in you; you are in Him. That is the sure fact of the Word of God.

When you're more conscious of your failure than you are of His sufficiency, everything grinds to a halt, even if you're more conscious of your failure to reach God. Worship, love, dependency, supply—all get backed up as in a clogged drain. You must become more conscious of His sufficiency than of your failure for the spiritual process to restart.

Make no mistake about it, humility does not cause you to be more conscious of your failure than of His sufficiency, pride does! Pride says it shouldn't be so. Humility says it will always be so but for the grace of God. Humility says your failure and need, not your deserts, qualify you for the grace of God now as any other time. What you need is His mercy!

About Those Feelings

Sometimes our biggest hindrance in prayer may be our feelings. On occasion these may be a result of the condition, not of our spirits, but of our bodies. For example, one of my most difficult, disappointing periods of prayer occurred recently. The only time I felt anything good happened was when I was largely asleep while seeking the Lord! But even after this, I felt terrible. No wonder! Within an hour, my dear wife was shocked to find me "as white as a sheet." I'd just come within a hair's breadth of passing out in the bathroom! I might be at peace, but she feared for my physical heart.

Feelings are certainly not to be depended on. In this sure knowledge is hope for those who suffer from mental illness, especially from nerve disorders that may be caused by a chemical imbalance in the physical system.

We need to beware of depending at all on feelings, so readily can they be the enemy of faith. We're so easily snared by bad feelings, and almost equally by good feelings—the good feelings we too often covet instead of Him.

Regardless of feelings, He is in you, and you are in Him! You have a right to trust Him and rest in Him. He's the all-sufficient supply of all you need. None of these truths are dependent on the presence of feelings. Why should we live by changing feelings when we can live by the changeless reality?

What More Can You Do?

Seek to worship Him, not with mere words, nor just abstractly, but as what and who you need right now. To do otherwise is sometimes to play word games of pretense, which could be part of the reason for your failure to communicate with the God of truth and reality.

Let the Lord show you where you're not pleasing Him. Let Him deal with whatever it is

He reveals as displeasing until it's happily settled between you. Let Him reveal your worries and fears, your mistrust of Him. Agree with Him about them. Allow Him to change them. Admit your wandering, loveless heart. Sincerely mourn over it if God enables you to.

Thank and praise Him for who He is and what He does, even when you don't feel at all like doing it.

Read the Word. Let it search and instruct you. Soak up Philippians 4:4-13. Let the Lord use it to make prayer in all its aspects and genuine heart submission real to you.

Write whatever comes to your mind that reflects where you're really at in your responses to the Lord right at that moment. The sense of failure may disappear as you see in black and white before you the evidence of your seeking heart.

Lay down in His arms. If you go to sleep there, be less concerned than if you continue to strive too long in agitated prayer.

At any point, under the Lord's direction, be prepared to turn your attention from your relationship with the Lord to genuine, heart-intercession for others. When Job did this, He found Himself freed. So may you. Sometimes, while I think it should be the opposite, I find my heart becoming sensitive to the Lord after times of loving intercession for others. God uses it to free me from my self-centeredness.

CHAPTER 13

The Emptying

*But God has chosen the foolish things
of the world to put to shame the wise;
and God has chosen the weak things
of the world
to put to shame the things which are mighty;
and base things of the world
and the things which are despised,
God has chosen,
and the things which are not,
to bring to nothing the things that are.
—1 Corinthians 1:27-28*

I was startled one morning to rediscover something of the deep blessing of earlier quiet times. I share this occurrence with you now, not that you may seek to emulate it, but to illustrate some of the thoughts I've expressed.

A Special Experience

I'd spent more time sleeping during about two hours with the Lord than I had actively communing with Him. Still, even in my sleep my heart was seeking Him.

As the time approached to begin my day's work, I longed for Him. Suddenly and unexpectedly, I found myself being emptied. A quiet joy filled me as He became all to me, and my independent self nothing. What had happened?

My spirit had come to the place of choosing God over all else. I wanted nothing but Him. I sought nothing but Him. I clung to nothing but Him. He was Lord of all. Anything that might try to supersede or supplant Him was repulsive. I wanted to give up and give over everything to Him.

Earlier on occasion, I had experienced the sense of my being entirely united with Him, lost in Him. Even though this was not the same, I was unconcerned. As long as I received more of Him and He more of me, my desires were totally met.

I was weak, gladly so, that His life might work in me. I was quieted because the striving vanished.

My self-will was gone, along with my selfish independence, self-conceit, fears, anxiety, and my need to be or do anything. My life was of no particular interest to me, because it was swallowed up in Him.

Tears flowed. He was there filling that emptiness with Himself, though I could scarcely believe He would fill such an unworthy vessel.

I wondered why I seemed to carry a pain with me into the start of the day. Then I realized it was quite literally broken-heartedness over my inner rebellion against God. I was grief-stricken that I could want to be independent from my Creator and God. My rebellion seemed horrible to my broken spirit. I was humbled, gentled, made tender, sensitive, and responsive to the Lord and toward others.

The restlessness, the demands, the pressure were reduced. Any sign of their presence produced a hurt in my heart that was already aching with the breaking and emptying and the desire that it continue. An intense reluctance to face people and circumstances that would reintroduce the strife into my heart and shame that anything should be able to do so flooded my heart.

Abrupt Endings

Why had I stopped experiencing such emptyings? Did God need to strip me of my pride in the special things He had done for me? Did He in His infinite wisdom know that a continuation of such experiences would deprive me of the humility I needed to learn to walk with Him?

Was I forgetting to let go and let God? Was I neglecting to relinquish everything to Him? Was I holding onto my control of my circumstances? Was I holding onto my right to things, needs, concerns, worries? Was I failing to let them all go to Him? In my heart of hearts did I want something more than having God in charge of everything for me?

Was it that in spite of my profession to accept everything the Lord sent my way as best for me, I really didn't? Though I thought it had improved, I was still frequently upset with people and circumstances. Such reactions are those of the world rather than of one who rests everything in His Lord. Inside I was still too often frustrated, angry, or fearful. At the time I thought the blame might lie especially with my failure to do as the Lord had asked and stop watching TV and overeating.

My Unwillingness to Trust Him

But I realized something very special that morning. No failure of mine needed to rob me of peace in the Lord unless it was willful. My unwillingness to trust the Lord with everything, including my failure, robbed me of Him. Having my eyes on myself rather than on the Lord incapacitated me to receive Him, His emptying, or anything else He wanted to give me.

The fact is that if I waited until I stopped failing my God altogether, I'd wait until eternity. Only by His grace do I receive any of His blessings, never by my deserving.

Sure, I often felt like a hypocrite for telling the Lord nothing mattered but Him, that I had no will but His, when I was continually failing to please Him in specific matters. But that morning I knew that just then I meant without reservation He was all that mattered. He had worked it within me. For that moment it was absolutely true, just as absolutely true as though I always lived fully by it.

This wasn't of my doing, but His. I could never do it. I could never empty myself. Only He could, even in spite of my failure. That's because my failure isn't the significant factor; His undeserved grace and mercy is.

Here we have come full circle, back to the place we started. We are qualified for His grace and mercy by our failure, and need, and sin!

Only by Him

All of this is God's work, not ours. Only the Lord can make genuine heart-seeking of Him possible. Only He can bring us to the place of actual heart-surrender. If we attempt it, we have nothing but empty words without meaning.

Instead, we present ourselves before Him in His merit alone with nothing in our hand but our need. Then we wait there for Him to work as He will.

We want to let go of our control of everything. We want to relinquish it all to Him in quiet meekness, trust, and confidence. We want to, whether we have the moral capacity to do it or not. We recognize that He can do all that we cannot. That's all. Then it's up to Him to do as He will.

Any self-effort will only stand in the way, just as much as will any self-dependence or anything else of self.

Not an Experience, But a Reality

Please don't seek this experience, or any other. Instead seek the Lord. Praise Him. Worship and adore Him. The seeking of any experience with God can be a form of idolatry—putting something ahead of the Lord Himself.

However, simply being willing to let God empty you of yourself and fill you with Himself will bring blessing. The emptying, the becoming needy, hopeless, and helpless are still as much key to all our responses to Him as they were in chapter one. It will never change!

We're often told to surrender all to Jesus. So we try to do it as a choice, a decision generated by our own will-power, but we find ourselves disappointed. When we're emptied and broken-hearted, poor and needy, He has already effected the surrender.

We're told we must be humble, and we find we're anything but. When we're emptied and broken-hearted, poor and needy, humility is no longer something we seek but something we experience.

We're told to rest and be at peace. Instead we find ourselves troubled and distressed. When we're emptied and broken-heartedly dependent on Him alone, His peace and rest are ours.

When we're emptied of ourselves, our attention goes spontaneously to Him. Or is it more accurately, when our attention goes to Him, we're spontaneously emptied of ourselves? In either case, when He works His emptying, breaking, drawing work within, it's done! What He does, He does well.

Many Christians won't spend enough time alone with the Lord to have their hard hearts softened, made tender toward God, and brought to the place of surrender by His Spirit. They won't let God tear down their idols so that He may reign supreme and alone. They won't let go of everything to Him. They won't relinquish their control of their affairs into His charge. Their innate rebellion, resistance, and resentment continue to grip them in a throttle-hold.

Emptied to Be Filled

Without the emptying—the breaking of our willful hearts—we live in strife without peace, for within ourselves is only constant strife.

The wicked are like the troubled sea,
when it cannot rest,
whose waters cast up mire and dirt.
"There is no peace," says my God,
"for the wicked."
—Isaiah 57:20-21

Often turn from yourself and toward Him. Worship and adore Him. Let Him empty you of all your independence. I've experienced both the quiet, beautiful benefits of such emptying and the sad consequences of missing it.

We must be emptied of our independent, rebellious selves to be filled with the Lord and His Spirit. I can't assure you of any other way of increasing dependence on the Lord than by being increasingly emptied of yourself. Without this we're driven to do. Do, in strife. Do, in fear. Do, out of necessity. Do, under pressure. Do, without peace, rest, and quiet meekness of spirit. Do, in self-reliance rather than in dependence on God.

My friend, God has something better for us than that. He offers Himself to do for us what we are incapable of doing.

CHAPTER 14

The Golden Secret

*Come to Me, all you who labor
and are heavy laden, and I will give you rest.
Take My yoke upon you, and learn from Me,
for I am meek and lowly in heart,
and you will find rest for your souls.
For My yoke is easy and My burden is light.*
—Matthew 11:28-30

*There remains therefore a rest
for the people of God.
For he who has entered His rest
has himself also ceased from his [own] works.*
—Hebrews 4:9-10

*Let the peace of God rule in your hearts,
to which also you were called in one body;
and be thankful.*
—Colossians 3:15

What is the secret of a Christianity that really works? *The golden secret is simply Jesus, and resting meekly and contentedly at peace in Him.*

We've been repeatedly told it, but have we heard it? Do we believe it? Have we received it? Have we begun to live it? Oh, that we might remain always patiently resting meekly and quietly in Him and His love.

If only we'd been able to do so from the beginning, years of spiritual barrenness and wanderings might have been avoided. God might from the start have been working His transforming work without our interference.

A Minister's Tale of Failure

A pastor in California had just read my original article in *The Christian World Report* entitled, *Do You Want a Christianity that Really Works?* This dear brother tearfully told me how he ached for a Christianity that works. After twenty years in the ministry, he'd run out of hope. He had tried everything—all the books, all the formulas. He was a spiritual failure. He had spent the previous year telling people how important it was that they make their chief goal knowing the Lord, but he hadn't been able to himself—at least not like he wanted to.

I sought to reveal to him the God of peace and hope. After introducing his congregation to this God that evening and watching them respond, he told me he'd never experienced anything like it. Every part of his life had been affected. But I had to warn him not to look to me, to experiences, or to knowledge—just to the Lord alone.

What More Could You Ask?

Many of us may be unprepared even yet to understand this secret with enlightened spiritual understanding. In spite of his desire, I'm not at all sure this dear, hurting brother was! Was he looking for the Lord or for something to fix his hurt and fill his need?

What more could any human being ask for than the Lord, and with Him *"the rest"* that *"remains for the people of God"* (Hebrews 4:9), *"the peace of God which surpasses all understanding"* (Philippians 4:7)? You could have friends, popularity, pleasure, pride, intelligence, knowledge, wisdom, wealth, health, good looks, and exquisite taste. You could have these and much more and still live in constant distress, scarcely ever knowing a moment of rest of mind and heart, of inner peace. What would they all be worth? It's a wise man who will trade everything of this life for God, and with Him peace or rest of heart.

But it's not just that we might be spared so much unnecessary distress that the Lord so fully and freely offers us, with Himself, His rest. It's especially that, as we rest contentedly at home in Him, and only then, is He able to give us more of Himself. There's no other venue in which He can so generously reveal Himself to us, unveil Himself to us, give Himself to us, as that of rest and peace.

When we come to Him for Himself alone, He gives us not only Himself, but the best there is beside Him—His own free gift of rest. As we remain in Him and in His rest so freely given, He *"with Him also freely give[s] us all things"* (Romans 8:32). We don't have to do a thing but turn and return to Him in peace and rest to receive His free gifts in abundance. No matter what our activity in response to His love call, that activity can be engaged in without the necessity of disrupting our peace, our rest, our contentment in Him.

All our lives we can just continue resting content in Him and receiving Him, His very life, and all His good things. To substitute some other way of our own is to end in frustration and failure.

To Abide Is To Remain in His Rest

First, read John 15:1-17. The abiding in Christ described in this familiar passage is just this same remaining contentedly in Him and His love.

As we continue resting in Him, He freely provides for us, without any merit or effort on our part, His own life abundantly working in

us. He gives us His life not only to meet the
needs of every part of our lives but to produce
the fruit from which others may eat and live.

Again, what is this great secret? Please
don't be misled in thinking that it is just rest
and peace. That would be of only limited benefit. It is, of course, as always, the Lord Himself.
What more could we possibly ask?

He is always a secret mystery that is being
revealed or unveiled increasingly to our seeking spirits. As we turn to Him and remain in
Him in the spirit of His quiet meekness, He
best brings us Himself, and with Himself His
rest and His peace.

That is the message of the verses at the
beginning of the chapter. Why not take time
right now to read them again? Meditate on
them. Let the Spirit reinforce to your spirit the
wonderful liberating truth that as we come to
Him in our need, He makes us weak enough
and meek enough that He can reveal Himself
to us. To our weakness and meekness He can
give Himself, His life, His rest, His peace, and
all else we need.

The Enemy

One of the unsuspected enemies that
destroy our loving, trusting relationship with
the Lord is the pressure and hurry fed by fear.
Fear is in turn fed by lack of genuine trust in

God's ability to take care of everything for our benefit without any interference from us.

Our part is to rest contentedly, quietly, meekly in Him, His love, and His doing. In that quiet contentment we can freely receive whatever He wants to give. Even after we've learned it, we always tend to forget this: our struggling and striving only causes us and those around us unnecessary distress and grief. It hampers our fellowship with the Lord and His ability to give Himself more fully to us in love, and with Himself, *"all things,"* as He so longs to do.

Which Will it Be?

Quite possibly the most important question we can ask ourselves moment by moment is this: are we abiding in Him in rest and peace? On the other hand, are the sins of worry, doubt, disobedience, or mistrust, or even of unnecessary, unproductive hurry robbing us of Him and His rest and peace?

Let it not be, dear one. The price is too high. It's the constriction of the flow of the life of the omnipotent God in our poor needy lives.

Relax!

You will keep him in perfect peace,
whose mind is stayed on You,

because he trusts in You.
—Isaiah 26:3

And the work of righteousness will be peace,
and the effect of righteousness,
quietness and assurance forever.
—Isaiah 32:17

Our great sin is a wrong attitude toward God and toward ourselves: putting our trust in ourselves instead of in Him! The crazy part is that even though we know it doesn't work, we persist in clinging to our self-lives.

Deep down inside, we know we're not to be trusted. We know there's so very little we're capable of handling to our own satisfaction. This incapacity produces tensions of all kinds that are wearing and destructive.

Tension

We assume self-imposed responsibilities God never asked us to handle. We give ourselves deadlines in which God has no part. When there are deadlines of His permission, we add to them all kinds of things He hasn't. Then we fear we won't meet them. We don't rest with Him the legitimate responsibilities He permits us to have.

We don't deal openly with Him about our failures, producing still more internal tension.

143

We are scared to come to grips with the fact that we are going to fail God, ourselves, and others. We can confess our sin to God, admit contritely to others our hurtful failures, and seek by God's grace not to repeat them. But what do we do when we fail again?

Uncertainties also cause tension. Am I right or wrong? Did I do right or wrong? Did I make the right choice? What is going to happen next? For many of these life-shaping questions, we simply do not have the answers.

Give Them All to Him

In a world of this kind, can we really have rest of mind and spirit? Yes, we can—more than we ever dreamed—if we're willing to believe it is safe to rest every concern with the God of love. He's in the business of taking care of us with all our circumstances, with all our responsibilities, and even with all our sins, failures, and uncertainties.

What do we have to do to benefit from His willingness to take care of it all? Nothing! Just let Him. Just get out of the way and let it all go into His care, even our failures and uncertainties, even our sins. He is the only one capable of forgiving, cleansing, and transforming. All He asks is our willingness to agree with Him, call our sins "sins," and trust Him to act on them in His own power.

If we can't release our failure to Him as soon as we recognize it, our failure becomes an unbearable burden. This burden may be more destructive than all our fears and worries over external circumstances. Without excusing carelessness and willful disobedience, we are once more putting the initiative where it belongs, in the hands of our almighty God. It's only to exchange our meddling insufficiency for His all-sufficiency.

An Open Heart and Countenance

To function as fully as God intends, openness of heart and of countenance toward God and man are essential. We must rip away our masks, so nothing is false, nothing pretended. We need to become real, true, and transparent primarily toward God, but also toward man as a result. Anything contrary to the truth must be acknowledged and turned from.

The more complete are our openness and honesty, the more the freedom, peace, and joy. The opposite of the clamp-around-the-head, tightness-in-the-stomach syndrome, this is your right as a child of the King.

I put time and effort into helping a young man. Great progress was made—or was it? When the chips were down, he couldn't submit. At last I found out why. He had always denied committing a particular crime. Finally he admitted to me he had done it. He seemed to have gotten away with it, but he hadn't! He had caused himself and his family untold agony because he could not obey the Spirit's voice telling him to confess it. He wouldn't be open and real. The cost seemed too great! The last I knew, it still did.

Only *"the wicked are like the troubled sea, when it cannot rest, whose waters cast up mire and dirt. 'There is no peace,' says my God, 'for the wicked'"* (Isaiah 57:20-21). Let us not be named among them.

CHAPTER 15

Peace and Patience!

*I have learned, in whatever state I am,
to be content.
I know both how to be abased,
and I know how to abound.
Everywhere and in all things, I have learned
both to be full and to be hungry,
both to abound and to suffer need.
I can do all things through Christ
who strengthens me.*
—Philippians 4:11-13

Most mornings we are not awake for very long before something occurs we really dislike. We react negatively, resentfully, fearfully, angrily. We may think it doesn't show to the outside world, but we are already torn up internally.

We are discontented, upset, and unhappy. As the day goes on, frustration builds up until someone gets in our way, and then we let them know they're out of line! Somehow the littlest irritations produce the biggest reactions in us.

Oh, you don't act like that? Perhaps not overtly, but what goes on inside? You try to keep the emotions hidden, pretending they aren't there, which only compounds the hurt and the frustration you feel.

In addition are all the deadlines and demands that put us under so much pressure. We rush to get it all done, which just makes us more pressed and frustrated. As anxiety builds, we feel the tightness in the chest and the band around the head. Some of us get ulcers. All of us suffer, and so does everyone around us.

Where have our peace and happiness gone?

Another Environment

We are in Christ. Paul said, *"In Him we live and move and have our being"* (Acts 17:28). However unpleasant our circumstances, if we have received the Lord Jesus Christ as our personal Savior, we are in Him. He is our primary environment—to the extent we allow.

God wants to take care of all our concerns. There's no need of turning anywhere else for safety, security, or supply. In Him we can rest secure. God's control and timing are perfect, so we have no need to hurry or to be anxious.

Being in Him is enough. We need nothing else, nothing more. We can be entirely content in Him, our perfect environment. We can relax.

Instead of Hurry, Struggle, and Stress

We are so impatient, so demanding, so pushy that we push ourselves out of the way of God's good gifts, including Himself and His peace. The God to whom we need to give our loving, responsive, dependent attention in rest and peace is called *"the God of patience"* (Romans 15:5). He places more emphasis in His Word on patience than we remember.

Add to your faith virtue;
and to virtue, knowledge;
and to knowledge, temperance;
and to temperance, patience;
and to patience, godliness;
and to godliness, brotherly kindness;
and to brotherly kindness, love.
For if these things be in you, and abound,
they make you that ye shall
neither be barren nor unfruitful
in the knowledge of our LORD Jesus Christ.
—2 Peter 1:5-8 KJV

And not only so,
but we glory in tribulations also,
knowing that tribulation worketh patience;
and patience experience; and experience, hope;
and hope maketh not ashamed,
because the love of God is shed abroad
in our hearts by the Holy Ghost

which is given unto us.
—Romans 5:3-5 KJV

We need to let the Lord teach us to rest in Him in quiet confidence, to turn from the awful sin of impatient hurry, and to allow Him to be our patience and contentment. As we do, we'll spend less frustrated effort on trying somehow, and often fruitlessly, to give Him our loving, responsive attention. We'll come nearer that place of constant abiding in Him and His love.

Be sure of this: this rest is not to be found by a forced activity of the will, but rather through an unresisting receptivity directed to the omnipotent God *"in whom we live and move and have our being"* (Acts 17:28). He offers us His rest freely. All we can do is receive it. He said, *"My peace I give to you"* (John 14:27). It is the peace of God that *"surpasses all understanding"* (Philippians 4:7). God's peace comes to us only in Himself. He is our rest as He is all else.

Look away from the upsetting circumstance to the faithful God. Let Him release you from your bondage to that unacceptable thing. Look away to Jesus. Let all your panic subside in His loving presence. When it tries to resurface, don't fight it. Just look to Jesus again. In quiet trust and resignation of spirit, passively accept the difficult circumstances as within His perfect providence for you.

Don't try to find reasons or solutions for the trouble. Just know He is capably in charge of the situation, so you don't have to be! Leave it with Him to resolve in His time and way. Believe Romans 8:28 as fully as He enables.

So when you can do no more, just look to Jesus. In your pain, crawl up into the Father's loving arms. Let the negative responses dissolve in His caring. Let them be replaced by thankfulness that He is your God, loving, in charge, working everything for your good.

STOP!

Yes, STOP! Stop right where you are.
When you're mistreated, stop.
When they expect too much of you, stop.
When nobody cares, stop.
When you're imposed upon, stop.
When you hurt, stop.
When you're overwhelmed, stop.
When time is running out, stop.
When everything goes wrong, stop.
When you're anxious and worried, stop.
When you're sick, stop.
When you're tired, stop.
When you're frustrated, stop.
When you're angry, stop.
Whenever you realize you're rushing, stop!
When you stop, He's there for you. You're in Him. Right at that moment, you're in Him.

You're already where you want and need to be, so you need not go anywhere else.

Why look elsewhere, especially to ourselves? What arrogant stupidity to try to care for all our multitudinous concerns when He who is infinitely capable wants to take care of all of them for us? Why run around all uptight about things being out of our control, when they're never out of His control? After all, He did promise to work all things together for our benefit, didn't He?

This Is Victory

Christians are always looking for the elusive spiritual victory promised them, desperately searching for something that seems just out of reach.

Just quit! When you stop, He starts. Our God is a gentleman. In His grace, He will not elbow His way in where He isn't wanted. If you insist on taking care of everything yourself, He lets you try. Even though it pains Him that you choose to slight Him and hurt yourself, He allows you that choice.

When we try to care for things ourselves, when we won't stop to let Him take care of them for us, we show our mistrust of Him. We grieve His tender, loving heart. We suffer untold, unnecessary pain and distress.

When you stop, He starts. This is true victory. He is our victory as He is our life and all else we'll let Him be.

Is there anything so important you would rather grieve Him and live in torment than stop and let Him take control? Is there anything in all the world you can handle better than can God?

If there isn't, then begin now to stop on every reminder and just be there, in Him, for Him to take control. He will, the moment you stop and stay in Him in expectant trust, knowing He is in charge so you needn't be. Then you can continue in relaxed restfulness in Him, even while doing whatever you need to do, as He accomplishes His good purposes in your circumstances under His control. There you can rest in Him in easy thankfulness.

Stop Trying to Fix Your World!

This is more important than it sounds: by the Lord's enabling, leave others' follies as well as yours with the One in whose care they can be trusted. The horrid need to straighten people out is part of our desire to control.

Ultimately, we can't control our circumstances, and we certainly can't control or change other people. By God's grace, we can trust both to Him. Let Him be in charge. Only then can He guide us to any helpful action that will bring blessing into the situation.

Similarly, stop living to please people. Stop longing for their approval. Only so will you be able to live for His approval alone. To live for the approval of others is to live in constant distress. To live in the assurance of the Lord's approval by grace is constant joy.

For some of us these are huge changes! They are changes that, like all the others, only Christ in us is able to produce as His life becomes increasingly our life in actuality.

Peace Replaces Rebellion and Worry

Loving, worshipful attention to our trustworthy God brings peace. It brings peace in place of the worry, hurry, and flurry that visit such pain and frustration on the human race. God lives in the domain of peace. Whenever our peace flees, we must return to the God of peace. We then allow Him to continue His transforming work that has been interrupted.

As we spend quality love time with Him, as we gladly accept as His love-gift all the circumstances He sends our way, as we thank Him that He is giving us more of Himself in them, His peace is just one of the blessings He gives to us. The incapacity we feel to respond with spiritual rather than fleshly responses will gradually be replaced with a new capacity. His name will be honored in the whole process.

God's Timing

I want to emphasize the word *gradually* and remind you that, above all, you must seek the Lord with patience. Many of us are so rebellious, independent, self-reliant, and proud that it takes God years to get a significant amount of our attention. In my case, it was fifty-one.

For many of us it seems to take years more for our dependence to be transferred to Him from ourselves to any great degree. But in these years we slowly learn about patiently seeking Him and resting content in His love.

Patiently let the Lord have your positive, receptive, submissive attention. By faith, seek to sacrifice everything back to God with contentment and thanksgiving. Abandon yourself ever more into His loving care. Wait on Him in quietness and peace. Respond to Him as fully as He enables, withholding nothing from Him.

You may be disappointed at your slow pace and even perceived failure. Instead of wallowing in self-pity or returning to frustration and anger toward God, turn quietly to Him at every recognition of your failure and need.

Then watch Him, surely if slowly, draw you to Himself. Watch as He transforms you into His likeness. Watch as the fruit of the Spirit is spontaneously formed within and evidenced in your relationships with others.

Observe Him increasingly reaching out through you with His love, even to the unlovely. His love shed abroad in your heart will inexorably cause you to serve God and man even at personal sacrifice. It will cause you to want Him to draw others to Himself that they may be helped and He may praised.

CHAPTER 16

The Golden Key

*For those who live according to the flesh
set their minds on the things of the flesh,
but those who live according to the Spirit,
the things of the Spirit.
For to be carnally minded is death,
but to be spiritually minded is life and peace.*
—Romans 8:5-6

*Peace I leave with you,
My peace I give to you;
not as the world gives do I give to you.
Let not your heart be troubled,
neither let it be afraid.*
—John 14:27

*Now may the LORD of peace Himself give you
peace always in every way.
The LORD be with you all.*
—2 Thessalonians 3:16

*Now may the God of peace Himself
sanctify you completely.*
—1 Thessalonians 5:23

For every child of God, a golden key exists that can open the door to the golden secret of living in the Lord in rest and peace.

The Key

Remember that Christ is in you, your hope of glory. Remember that you are in Him where you can always rest, receiving His sufficient supply for all things. Withdraw in quietness from the outward, external things to rest meekly in Him. Let go of everything into His control. Whenever possible, allow your spirit to be drawn by Him into His peace. *The key to unlocking the door to restful living is simply turning again and again to Christ.*

Always Aim to Abide

The golden secret is constant residing and abiding in the Lord Himself in rest and peace. Let's always remember this ultimate objective. Let's not aim for anything less, no matter how short of it we may constantly seem to fall. If we could but remain peacefully at home in the Lord, we could always respond tranquilly to Him and to everything else, whether eternal and spiritual, or temporal and physical.

Yet, just because we don't always remain in His rest, the golden key is necessary. Far better would we be if we remained constantly, confidently abiding in the Lord and His love in rest and peace, receiving always of His life. But since we don't, we must return to our resting place in Him just as often and as quickly as we recognize that we've wandered.

Using the Key

Whether in your prayer closet, your car, office, garden, or kitchen, you can withdraw in quietness from things outward to rest contentedly in Him. Your heart simply abandons whatever has been occupying its self-centered attention to come quietly and meekly to God in your spirit to rest unresistingly in Him there. Just relinquish whatever has captured your attention that is neither God nor of Him.

You find yourself being drawn tranquilly to Him. He is the author of the quietness into which you are drawn. He is the author of the peace you find there.

You remain peacefully and quietly in Him as you remain in loving resignation to Him. Any self-seeking or resentment toward God, people, or your circumstances will return you to that outward realm of confusion and distress, as will failure to let go of everything to Him.

As you abide in a spirit of loving resignation to Him, an attitude of tender receptivity and expectancy toward your Lord of love will grow in your heart. You become more sensitive, loving, and pliable in His hands. His Spirit is able to accomplish in your spirit something more of what He wants, whatever its character may be. Beautifully, He does it with no real effort on your part as you rest trustingly in Him!

Learning to walk with God is in this respect very much like learning to walk physically. Whether we're one or ninety-one, walking is just picking one foot up and putting it down ahead of the other, and repeating that procedure again and again. We must keep at it no matter how often we fall. In our Christian walk, we want to get there by just picking our foot up and putting it down once, as it were. Doing it again and again is too tedious for our liking. Then we wonder why we fail.

Emotions, Intellect, and Spirit

Some might mistakenly think of this way of coming to the Lord in peace as an exercise of the emotions. To use this golden key to the golden secret properly doesn't depend on the emotions. The rest and peace we seek to live in is not so much a feeling as the absence of unnecessary stress. However, don't seek peace, but the God of peace. He alone can replace the idols that enslave us to stress and distress.

The golden key can be used by faith without feelings as an entrance to living and walking with God in our inner man. We may abide, remain, rest in Christ just as much when we have no particular feelings as when we do. We may find the greatest benefit from simply recognizing that we are in Christ, as He is in us, and resting in the reality of it, just because God says it's so.

Both emotionalism and intellectualism open us to delusion. So does any way we leave God out of the central place of our hearts.

Do you remember our goal? *The Lord is the desire of your heart, the focus of your attention, the object of your love.* Him we worship and adore. To Him we offer loving resignation and tender receptivity. To Him we withdraw from things outward and find rest for our spirits.

The only safe road to God is the road of humility, meekness, and need before His infinite perfection and holiness. This is the road we must take.

A New Mind

Please believe me, my friend. You can't work up a desire for God adequate to lead you to walk in Him and His peace. You can't simply make new demands on yourself that this time you will use the golden key to enter the realm of the golden secret. This is not a trick or gimmick to allow the self-centered to gain their way into the inner sanctum.

A new mind is required, the mind of Christ, that seeks harmony with God above all else. Only God can give us this inner desire for Him and for harmony with Him. The calmness, the openness of heart and of countenance that we have discussed doesn't stem from some action of our minds, emotions, or wills. Instead, God's work in our hearts and spirits settles as a quiet waiting on God in that inner domain of the spirit where He is in charge. There He is free to accomplish more and more of His perfect purposes without the interference of our independence, self-effort, or harried hurry.

The Flesh Seeks To Live On

The great deterrent to living in the golden secret is our unwillingness to die so our spirits may vibrate with the life of God. Apart from this effort of our independent selves to live on, dwelling in God in peace would be spontaneous and virtually effortless. Instead, we wander so unnecessarily alone.

However, we find restoration in the reality that Christ is in us, our life and all, and we are in Him, where we can rest contentedly at home, receiving His all-sufficient supply. In using this golden key, we turn in our spirits from ourselves and our circumstances to God.

Now, this may seem a strange way to follow the biblical advice to *"resist the devil and he will flee from you*" (James 4:7). But if we haven't yet learned that it's not really we who can effectively resist the devil, only He, we surely must. He acts on our behalf when we meekly, quietly trust in Him alone. He is our defense and our shield.

Cry "Abba, Father, Papa"

*As many as are led by the Spirit of God,
these are the sons of God.
For you did not receive the spirit
of bondage again to fear,
but you received the Spirit of adoption
by whom we cry out, "Abba, Father."*
—Romans 8:14-15

For this practice of using the golden key to become increasingly the habit of our lives, we need to be willing to respond to His call of Father-love enough to slow down and turn to Him repeatedly in quiet meekness of spirit. We need to let the Lord make us increasingly willing to forgo that which is neither His nor Him. We must allow Him to exchange fear for faith, dissolve mistrust into glad confidence, transform aggravation into gratitude. We must wait in growing quietness, meekness, and patience for His love to have its perfect work until our hearts begin spontaneously to cry,

"Father!" Surely for all the eternal benefit to be gained, this is a slight effort indeed.

Slow Down!

Many of us have lived all our lives in a hurry. To get anything done, or to do it well, I've had to put myself under pressure, or so I thought. I've had to really work at my work. Too often I felt the pressure in contrast to the peace that is my right from God.

To live in the golden secret of peace and rest in the Lord, we must slow down. To use the golden key requires that we take time throughout the day to commune quietly with Him, to have our hearts tuned to Him.

Unfortunately, our first response to everything is to try harder. This simply does not work with spiritual matters or in using the golden key. Instead of trying harder, the first response in every circumstance needs to be just to stop our struggling and striving.

When you stop and step back, you are able to turn your heart to the Lord in quietness and peace and relinquish everything to Him. Recall that Christ is in you, your hope of glory. Remember that you are in Him where you can always rest at home receiving His sufficient supply for all things. Withdraw then, whenever possible, in quietness from the earthly things to rest meekly and peacefully content in Him.

CHAPTER 17

Day by Day

Work out your own salvation
with fear and trembling;
for it is God which worketh in you
both to will and to do of his good pleasure.
—Philippians 2:12-13 KJV

We may find it strange if we discover that even having the golden key to the golden secret seems not to be enough to secure that closeness to the heart of God in love, rest, and peace that our renewed spirits long for. We may still find ourselves returning repeatedly to a sense of failure.

If we do, may we let our continuing failure merely reinforce our recognition that all is of God, nothing of ourselves. He alone is our hope. Nothing we think, do, or say is of any benefit or value whatever unless it is born of His Spirit and enabled and empowered by Him, not at this crucial point in our journey with God any more than it is at any other.

From the beginning we have chosen separation from God, not He from us. From the beginning He has sought us out and drawn us to Himself. It is He who continues to do so.

Still, we need to be reminded that this provides no room for spiritual laziness, carelessness, or irresponsibility on our part. The Spirit of God has placed within us the desire to live in holy harmony with Him. So He places within us the desire to do those things and maintain those attitudes that make it possible for us to avoid that which distances us from Him and maintain those attitudes that assist us to better respond to His drawing.

We Must Do the Responding

As we once responded to His dying love, so must we respond repeatedly to His living, undying love. Philippians 2:13 can't be separated from Philippians 2:12. It is the God who works in us to will and to do of His good pleasure who asks us to work out our own salvation with fear and trembling.

God does all He can to induce us to respond in love to Him. The one thing He won't do is respond for us. He has left that to us.

Burning the Trash

The God of love is also the God who is a *"consuming fire"* (Hebrews 12:29). Sooner or later to be purely love, He must consume or commit to eternal fire all in this universe that destructively resists His love and grace. Until He does, no restoration of universal love, joy, peace, longsuffering, gentleness, goodness, faith, meekness, and temperance can occur. Until He does, there can be only a continuation of the world's hurt, pain, agony, and anguish.

Always remember this: His love demands that all be made right in final judgment. But we need not wait for that day to receive many of the benefits of His love and end much of the pain attendant on refusing it.

Sins Aren't the Accident of Circumstance

The heart is deceitful above all things,
and desperately wicked; who can know it?
—Jeremiah 17:9

The Hebrew suggests that the heart is crooked and slippery, treacherous and untrustworthy, turned against God. Sins are a natural effect of the character of the unregenerate human heart, not simply the accident of circumstance. Sinful rebellion against almighty God remains the character of the old man of the flesh even in the redeemed child of God.

Positionally, the old man was crucified with Christ; but in everyday practice, something has to change. In the final analysis, this isn't something we can do. God must effect the change if it is to be accomplished.

The Lord must bring us to the end of our self-righteousness, self-effort, and self-dependence. In reality this comes only by the cross through pain, suffering, and death. Paul longed to *"know Him and the power of His resurrection, and the fellowship of His sufferings, being conformed to His death"* (Philippians 3:10). So must you and I.

God sends or allows in our lives troubles and trials, difficulties, sickness, separation, loneliness, financial loss and deprivation, loss of reputation, uncertainty, and failure. As we stop resisting and resenting these, as we accept them as His gifts of love, we become weak, needy, and dependent. In this is our hope.

His Strength in Our Weakness

Paul asked God to take away his thorn in the flesh only three times. Once the Lord had showed him it was sent for His eternal benefit, he stopped asking. As nearly as we know, he lived contentedly, even gratefully with it the rest of his life.

God told Paul, *"My grace is sufficient for you, for My strength is made perfect in weakness"* (2 Corinthians 12:9). To paraphrase, God was telling Paul, "If you want My strength, you're going to need to be constantly reminded of how weak you really are. If you're going to depend on Me, you're going to need to be reminded how futile it is to rely on yourself."

Paul accepted God's wisdom and chose to value the infirmities, reproaches, necessities, persecutions, and distresses the Lord permitted to be his. (See 2 Corinthians 12:10.) Paul realized it was only as he was made weak that his foolish, sinful heart was willing to take its life and strength from the Lord.

The God of all the universe waited within willingly, lovingly, longingly, to give Paul all he needed. Just so, He waits in us. May God enable us to make Paul's choice ours.

Hope Even for Us

Have you found it extraordinarily difficult to grasp what you've been reading so far? Has there seemed to be little desire in your heart to put it into practice? Perhaps you haven't yet been prepared by the humbling of your pride, the breaking of your stubborn rebel will. You haven't yet been brought down to a place of need sufficiently deep to desire what the Lord has for you in Himself whatever the cost.

Tell God it's so. Give Him permission to tear away all the crutches of the flesh and to make you really needy. Ask Him to create in you a nonresistance to what He sends your way, even the least humanly acceptable. Ask

Him that you may someday be able, by His grace, to welcome all that tears you from other loves than Him. Ask of Him grace that you may be able to begin hugging to your breast whatever He sends as His messengers of love.

Whatever the circumstances, He can teach you increasingly to accept them from His own good hand of love without resistance. He can enable you to thank Him that, in them all, He seeks ultimately to bring you more of Himself. As you lovingly yield to Him and His eternal purposes, He will give you Himself more fully.

Embracing Change

Let's remember that He is in us, our hope of glory, and that we are in Him where we can rest at peace as we embrace His transforming work. Let's give Him our attention. Let's withdraw peacefully into the chapel of our spirits, relinquishing all to Him. Let's remain there as much as possible, residing and abiding in Him, His love and peace, receiving of His life. Let's cast ourselves into His arms of love.

Let Him teach us to let Him have the place where He belongs—fully in charge of drawing us to Himself and of all else, too. Let Him teach us to take the place where we belong, trustfully at rest in Him, relying on Him to draw us to Himself and meet every need we have of whatever kind.

What Hinders?

Why do we try to make this our practice, yet continue to live still in so much failure?

Alone with the Lord, I was unhappily recognizing again my unsatisfactory level of obedience to Him. I realized that after all He had taught me about His absolute trustworthiness, my problem still was my feeble trust of Him. I was afraid of what might happen if I always obeyed Him. So I scribbled in my journal, "Everything God asks of me is good."

The consequences of obeying God are never bad! They are always good. They may sometimes be difficult or painful, but never bad.

Will I accept the difficult consequences, the painful consequences of obeying God? If not, I do not trust Him. I'll find myself yielding often to my will, rather than His, and to temptation. I'll be spiritually depleted and weak.

My heart must say, "Everything He asks of me, or ever could ask of me, is good. Anything He would take from me is bad for me, even if it seems good." Obeying Him then will be easier.

Every Thought a Prayer!

You may find a considerable asset in quietly, comfortably, yet earnestly, seeking to commune with the Lord throughout the day. We're constantly thinking and talking to ourselves. These conversations with ourselves don't generally tend to be filled with God, or love, or worship of Him or even with selfless concerns to benefit others. They are largely me-centered.

We talked earlier about the need of God getting our attention. You may have tried to turn more of your thoughts toward Him, but without much success. The main benefit may have been to show you how much you really want your own thoughts and your own way, rather than His. The result should be to cast you on Him to change this.

Trust Him, then, to place Himself increasingly in the center of your thought life. Let Him teach you to quietly converse with Him so habitually that every thought may become a prayer. Commit it to Him in quiet confidence that He will do it.

Then look to Him to see if He would have you apply yourself energetically to the practice. Be prepared under His direction to diligently seek to turn your thoughts, one by one, toward God. Be equally prepared for Him to direct you to rest in Him to do it.

You are uniquely His. He is uniquely yours. Let Him direct you uniquely. But be sure to ask Him to make you sensitively aware of His guidance. Let Him choose the means of putting Himself at the center of more and more of your thoughts until, at last, your thinking becomes truly praying.

Communion Based on Transformed Attitudes

Let Him change your selfish desires into unselfish ones, your self-centered thoughts into God-centered thoughts. May your communion and communication with Him become the reflection of transformed inner attitudes —attitudes that are loving, trusting, meek, unresisting, needy, dependent, receptive, quiet, and peaceful; attitudes that God works in us as we trust in Him to do it and accept His direction of our responses.

Remember that the more genuine, honest, and open this conversing with God becomes the better. Otherwise, even your conversation with God will tend toward selfishness and pretense, and will be filled with tension, worry, and fear. Becoming an obligation of the flesh, it will be a source of bondage rather than the glorious liberty of the sons of God.

However little your progress may seem to be in seeking to turn from conversing with yourself to conversing with your Lord, never relinquish it as a vital goal. Keep it before you in rest and peace. But if it comes to a choice, let there be no contest—above all focus on Him, His praise, His glory, His rest, and His peace.

CHAPTER 18

Dynamic Life Out of Constant Death

That I might live to God.
I have been crucified with Christ:
it is no longer I who live,
but Christ lives in me;
and the life which I now live in the flesh
I live by faith in the Son of God,
who loved me and gave Himself for me.
—Galatians 2:19-20

Reckon yourselves to be dead indeed to sin,
but alive unto God
in Christ Jesus our LORD.
Therefore do not let sin reign
in your mortal body,
that you should obey it in its lusts.
And do not present your members
as instruments of unrighteousness to sin,
but present yourselves to God
as being alive from the dead,
and your members
as instruments of righteousness to God.
—Romans 6:11-13

174

During a discussion period of a class I was conducting on new life in Christ Jesus, an active church member suggested that death to self was the key. My response was that indeed it could be if it were more than theology and theory. That person never attended another session! Later it became evident that the same individual had been living in unconfessed sin.

Few of us adequately understand the significance of the cross in our daily lives. At the cross our Lord Jesus Christ dealt sin its death blow. This is no less true than as though it were already fully evidenced—as it some day shall be by sin's total annihilation.

When we first accepted His finished work for us, we accepted the death blow for all sin in us. We died to any right to independence from God that we ever claimed or supposed we had. Of course, we little realized it then! But the question now is whether we have fully accepted this fact: I died with Christ.

False Freedom

Could our internal reaction secretly be, "How terrible that I can't be independent!"? Oh, what fools we are! Can we actually want to be independent from God? Why? What do we expect to gain? Freedom from God, of course.

How could we desire freedom from an all-loving, all-caring, all-sufficient, infinitely perfect God? What kind of freedom is that? The freedom to continue in the pain and agony, the guilt and torment, the heartache and distress, the uncertainty and disillusionment, the alienation and loneliness that separation from God has visited on the whole human race—and very personally on me—isn't very free. Surely only a twisted mind could want it, a mind twisted by inner enslavement to sin in the name of freedom from God.

Whenever we reassert a supposed right to some independence from the Lord, we grieve His Spirit and limit His working in us. But it isn't only God we grieve; it is also ourselves. We harm many others, too—not only our family and friends, but that significant section of the human race that our extended influence eventually reaches. We've foolishly and destructively reclaimed our supposed right to independence from almighty God as though that were a battle we could actually win!

Liberty in Enslavement

True liberty is in our willing enslavement to Him. Our hope is in utter hopelessness in ourselves, joyous hope in Him alone.

Inadequacy is an asset, not a liability, so at last we may be cast on Him. His adequacy is in His life. Ours is in our death, that we might gain His life. Our hope is to stop looking to ourselves, depending on ourselves. Our hope is to begin joyously looking to and depending on our wonderful Lord.

Now, when it comes right down to daily practice, what is the resource I turn to in every need, myself or the Lord Jesus? What and whom do I draw upon?

When almighty God is willing to be my source and resource for everything, why should I be foolish enough to choose anything less? Oh, that in everything we would just cast ourselves joyously and hopefully on Jesus.

Singleness of Heart to God

We no longer occupy the position of slaves to our own foolish, sinful independence from God. We died with Christ to sin in us so that its claim on us is forever finished. We need, first, to stand on that encompassing deliverance in newness of life: In Christ I died to any right to any independence. For this reality to function, I must accept its relevance for me in every here and now. I no longer have the right to choose what I will do, only to seek to discover what the Lord wants so that, by His enabling, I might joyously do nothing else.

We might just as well settle right now whether we're going to continue to claim a supposed right to independence from God, or whether we'll recognize we have no such right.

A double minded man is unstable
in all his ways.
—James 1:8 KJV

Something in us wants so desperately to please God without having to relinquish our supposed right to the selfish desires of the flesh. My friend, it simply can't be done.

The Choice Should Be Obvious

Choose for yourselves this day
whom you will serve.
—Joshua 24:15

Let your life's attitude increasingly become all for Jesus and nothing for myself separate from Him. Our supreme life-goal is to please and glorify our majestic, loving, Creator. He alone is worthy. Whether we like it or not, we aren't worthy of any attention.

Let's learn that to the extent we live to please Him, we die to our self-pleasing. To the extent we live to please ourselves, we die to Him and His realm.

Rather than running frightened from the very thought of dying to our selfish pleasures and desires, let's pray that God will enable us to look for opportunities to die to all that is not of Him. So may we live to all that is of Him.

That's a tall order! More accurately, it's impossible, at least for our independent selves. But *you are not in the flesh but in the Spirit, if indeed the Spirit of God dwells in you* (Romans 8:9). Besides, we've already died with Christ to sin. All that remains is for us to look away from ourselves to Him, His peace, and His provision.

Grace Is Free

Every step in grace is a free gift from God. Why, then, do we say its cost is the relinquishing of all that is not Him? How dare we call such a great boon and blessing a cost?

Let us long for the day when we're able at last to look eagerly for prices we may gladly pay to follow Jesus. For surely we'll grow in the Lord and His love only so far as we're willing to pay what looks like a price to our independent selves. If you're not yet ready for this, will you make it your prayer that God will do whatever He must to bring you to the place of saying from your heart that you have no right whatever to any independence from God?

We may feel a certain sadness at this death. But this sadness is only part of the disgusting old man, the alien outer man, the rebel flesh. After all, he does not want to die. But this sadness of the independent self is the route to that joy of the Spirit that is our right.

Dead Reckoning

What does it mean to reckon ourselves to be dead indeed to sin? As simply stated in Romans 6:11-14, it means that we are to recognize the reality that, as Christ died for our sin, in our place in Him we died to sin. We are to accept the fact that, as a result, we need no longer to be victimized by sin.

Now, it's clear from this that we still have a problem with sin. If it were already obvious to all that sin had no place in our lives, there would be no need of recognizing, accepting, or reckoning on our place of victory.

There is a second half to this directive on reckoning. It's that we reckon ourselves *"to be alive to God in Christ Jesus our LORD."* Again it is simply that we recognize the reality that in Jesus Christ we are alive to God and all His power for us.

The passage goes on to tell us not to let sin reign in our mortal bodies so we obey their unholy desires, nor to yield our bodily parts as tools that unrighteousness can use as it wills. Oh, you say, "See, we do have to take charge and make the changes. I knew it all the time."

Well, not quite. Knowing our tendency to works, Paul goes on to tell us: yield yourselves to God—let go of your self-centered desires to Him, as one who is alive in Christ, and yield your bodily parts to Him to be tools of His righteousness—let go of your right to direct them for selfish purposes.

What are you being asked to do? Surrender your right to control yourself and your bodily parts for your own selfish purposes. Relinquish the right of control into the hands of God to do with them as He will. Leave it all with Him to provide His victory.

Now, this includes leaving it to Him to do His work in us at His pace, in His time, in His way. Often His way isn't ours. It takes more time than we like. Because we don't see His working, we stop trusting and resting in Him to complete the work. We try our way and fail, or we give up altogether. Again, we miss the blessing and the victory.

This relinquishing everything into His control in rest and peace is also the way we most effectively mortify or put to death the deeds of the body. We are led by the Spirit of God into new dimensions of victory as we rest in our relationship with our Father God and His Son, our Savior (Romans 8:4-17).

The way of works is the way of *"bondage again to fear"* (Romans 8:15). The way of relinquishing and resting is the way of life and glory. When you choose, choose well. There is more at stake than you can dream!

CHAPTER 19

Applying the Cross

And there went great multitudes with Him.
and He turned and said to them,
"If anyone comes to Me
and does not hate his father and mother,
wife and children, brothers and sisters,
yes, and his own life also,
he cannot be My disciple.
And whoever does not bear his cross
and come after Me
cannot be My disciple."
—Luke 14:25-27

By depriving me of the ministry I had been building for more than fifteen years, God started me seriously seeking Him. We could shortly have been without a car or home. But He had me at last where He wanted me, with my back to the wall. The culmination of about seventeen years of His efforts had brought me to my knees.

When God gave me a new ministry, He put some extraordinary demands on me. I could no longer ask for financial support, incur debt, or issue tax-deductible receipts. Yet, He saw us through the financial impossibilities in most miraculous ways, and He continues to do so.

At one point, it seemed like He sent a financial windfall. A supporter financed a place for me in a sales operation that seemed tailor-made for me. The dream of publishing large numbers of books calling God's people to Himself in love mushroomed.

Then God said, "No."

I couldn't quite believe He said it. So He had to tell me again and again. But how I praise Him that, in this instance, all I really wanted was to be as sure as possible of what He wanted so I could do it. I felt He was asking me to throw away a fortune, but that didn't really matter. I only desired to do what He wanted and do it gladly just to please Him.

The idea of applying the cross scarcely seemed relevant. Obedience came so easily, considering what I thought I was giving up. What was truly being reflected was the way the cross had already been applied to my life in the struggle of the previous five years, and my quest to know Him for Himself alone.

I Struggle, Too

I confess it isn't always like this. I've wrestled for years with being glued to the television. I believed that all spiritual life and victory was of the Lord Himself, none of me. As I struggled with my TV addiction, I frequently told Him I was hopeless and helpless. I repeatedly owned that if anything was going to be done, He would have to do it.

But my deliverance was still incomplete. I watched TV drama much less frequently. I tried to remember that He will share my love with no idol. But over and over I returned to watching when I had promised Him I would not.

The Way of Escape

No temptation has overtaken you
except such as is common to man;
but God is faithful,
who will not allow you to be tempted
beyond what you are able,
but with the temptation
will also make the way of escape,
that you may be able to bear it.
Therefore, my beloved,
flee from idolatry.
I speak as to wise men;
judge for yourselves what I say.
—1 Corinthians 10:13-15

Our Lord has made the way of escape through the blood of His cross. We are free in Him and the power of His death and His

184

resurrection life in us. In each new temptation He makes a way of escape by revealing to the sensitive heart the sin into which it is being led, and Himself, our way of escape.

Thus, the cross is applied to each particular temptation or situation. As we carry on in His comfort, His joy, and His victory, He enables us to seek Him and His eternal praise rather than our short-term pleasure.

But many times we simply are morally incapacitated even to take Him as our way of escape. Instead, in spite of our wishes for it to be otherwise, we try to find a way out ourselves and, of course, end in failure.

So it was with me and TV. Finally He just reached down and touched me! He scared me to death that I dared to tempt Him so. At last I was delighted to take His way out.

Just so, every deliverance must be of the Lord alone, never from us in any measure if it is to be real deliverance. He must do it His way, not any other, but He must do it!

Idolatry Hasn't Ended

Now these things became our examples,
to the intent that we should not lust
after evil things as they also lusted.
And do not become idolaters
as were some of them. As it is written,
"The people sat down to eat and drink,

and rose up to play."
Nor let us commit sexual immorality,
as some of them did,
and in one day twenty-three thousand fell;
...Now all these things happened
to them as examples,
and they are written for our admonition,
on whom the ends of the ages have come.
Therefore let him who thinks he stands
take heed lest he fall.
—1 Corinthians 10:6-8, 11-12

At heart, temptation is always an issue of idolatry or of the covetousness the Bible says is idolatry. (See Colossians 3:5.) Idolatry is putting something ahead of God in importance or wanting something God doesn't want for us.

Why doesn't He want us to have certain things? Because they aren't good for us!

Our problem from the beginning has been our covetous, idolatrous lust for things other than the Lord Himself and what He knows is good for us. This idolatry brought the Old Testament kingdoms of Israel and Judah to their downfall. They often sought to cling to the Lord and their idols, to please the Lord and themselves. We must learn it isn't possible.

Let's not be foolishly misled, either, into blaming God deep within for our failure. He is everything we need. All we have to do is to turn to Him from the tempting goodies the evil one holds out to us.

Cast yourself on Him. Let Him, not your will, backbone, or self-discipline, be your hope. If you find yourself morally incapacitated to let go of the thing to which you so foolishly cling, don't abuse yourself. Instead, humbly admit your inability. Cast yourself on Him all the more. Be assured that ultimately His victory will be yours.

Finding Our Standards

If we look to the church for our model of conduct rather than to the Word and the Spirit, we'll frequently find little encouragement to apply the cross to our covetous idolatries. The Word admonishes us not to be conformed to the world, but the church generally fails to respond. Church people look much like their counterparts without Christ. They think like them in so many ways. They value so many of the same things. They have so many of the same practices and habits. Those who would really be different for Christ's sake are often oddballs even within the church.

No better picture exists in the Scriptures of what God would have us to be than that found in the third chapter of Colossians. I urge you to get your Bible and read it with prayer.

The opening verses admonish us to give our attention to things above where Christ is at the right hand of the Father. Then we're counselled to put to death our covetous idolatry that brings God's wrath on the lost. Next we're urged to put off the old man with his deeds and put on the new man. After the command to let the peace of God rule in our hearts, we're told to let the word of Christ dwell in us richly, teaching and admonishing one another with psalms, hymns, and spiritual songs, doing all in the name of Jesus with thanksgiving.

Look at all this realistically. How do you expect to give your attention to newspapers, radio, and TV more than to the written Word of God and still be able to let the word of Christ dwell in you richly? How do you expect to listen to the world's music and minister to yourself and others with songs, hymns, and spiritual songs? How do you expect to do everything in Jesus' name with thanksgiving when you spend your time with the greed, ugliness, self-centeredness, violence, lust and immorality of TV, or in idle talk, crass jokes, or grumbling with family and friends?

The Poisonous Sweet Tooth

I'm reminded of people who develop a sweet tooth. They become addicted to sugars. They're being physically poisoned by their passion for sweets, as their taste for healthy foods such as fruits and vegetables is eroded.

Just so, Christians who feed their passions for the things of this world lose their desire for the things of the world to come. I beg you to stop seeing how much of this world you can hold onto and still be a good Christian. Instead, see how many of the things of this world you can let drop out of your life, in preference for Him who is your life.

Filling our minds with the world's words and works is putting back on the old man. Surely his deeds will follow!

Don't Stop Short

One of the old writers who has helped me said many start down the road to close intimacy with our Lord only to fall short of their goal because they stop short of applying the cross to their lives. May this not characterize you or me! May we turn to the Lord, letting Him apply the cross to our idolatry. *"Therefore, my beloved, flee from idolatry. I speak as to wise men; judge for yourselves what I say"* (1 Corinthians 10:14-15).

At Peace with the Cross

The key blockage that needs to be unstopped, if we're to find a Christianity that really works, is our self-pleasing in all its forms. We need to be willing to let Him make us willing to forsake all to follow Him.

No salvation exists apart from the cross. Christ could not escape the cross and come forth in resurrection life, nor can we. The cross is the crux, the crucial point. We must deny ourselves, die daily, and take up our cross if we would follow Christ. We can't escape the cross and live in newness of life. If we choose ourselves and our way, we decide with death and destruction against life. The cross must be laid like an ax to the root of the tree. The cross must be applied to our every desire.

How does this coordinate with just living at rest in Him? Rest follows the cross; it does not precede it. *" 'There is no peace,' says the LORD, 'for the wicked'"* (Isaiah 48:22). Even Jesus sat down in rest only after He had gone to the cross:

For the joy that was set before Him,
[Jesus] endured the cross,
despising the shame,
and has sat down at the right hand
of the throne of God.
—Hebrews 12:2

Let there be no mistake. Conviction, repentance, confession, and restitution are followed by peace and rest, not the reverse.

But then we come full circle. Anything that robs us of peace and rest and joy in our Lord must go. Apply the power of the cross to it. Let God in His grace cross it out.

Let there come an end to defending any attitude of self-pleasing. We're full of wants that aren't of God, covetousness that is idolatry. Food, fun, fantasy, pleasure, and passion —be willing to let God deliver you even from your slavery to these. Then you can live at peace in Him—content to live not after the desires of the flesh, but after the desires of the Spirit.

CHAPTER 20

Walking in Liberty

*For the kingdom of God is not meat and
drink, but righteousness and peace
and joy in the Holy Spirit.
...Let us therefore pursue the things
which make for peace and the things
by which one may edify another.
Do not destroy the work of God
for the sake of food.
All things indeed are pure, but it is evil
for the man who eats with offence.
It is good neither to eat meat
nor to drink wine
nor anything by which your brother stumbles
or is offended or is made weak.
Do you have faith?
Have it to yourself before God.
Happy is he who does not condemn himself
in what he approves.
But he who doubts is condemned
if he eats, because he does not eat from faith;
for whatever is not from faith is sin.
—Romans 14:17, 19-23*

I trust you're seeing some real changes both inside and out. I hope you're responding increasingly to the desire God has put in your heart to live moment by moment in as close harmony as possible with Him: centering your focus on Him, worshiping Him, communing with Him, letting Him teach you to love and trust Him, relying on Him to bring good to you through every circumstance of life, rejecting any claim of the flesh to independence from Him, repeatedly turning inward to Him in rest and peace until you learn to abide in Him continually, dying to all that is not Him, accepting His power to give you new desires and responding to them by that same divine power, and seeking to relinquish all else that you might have Him more fully.

Hopefully, your focus and love is shifting away from yourself and the things of this life to Him. He can then draw you into His rest and peace, causing the struggles to abate, the fears to diminish, and your needs to be met in Him. You then become willing to be nobody apart from Him, immersed in Him and His love, seeking His praise rather than your pleasure.

Be Sensitively Responsive

Let's seek to respond sensitively to every sign of the new desires that the Lord gives us: desires to be drawn close to Him, to please

Him, to honor and glorify Him, to live only for Him and what is eternal and spiritual. Let's be increasingly prepared to pay the price of obedience: repeatedly rejecting the claim of our flesh to independence from Him.

If we're concerned that any habit or practice we permit in our lives doesn't please the Lord, we need to seek His help to lay it on the altar. Yes, the golden secret of a Christianity that really works is resting in the Lord and His peace so He is free to do His work in us. But surely it's obvious that God's work in us will be greatly hampered unless we let Him teach us and enable us to do less and less often what we know displeases Him, and more and more often what pleases Him.

Deliverance and Direction

We can know more of His deliverance from even those things of which we're in doubt, for *"whatever is not from faith is sin."* At the same time, we can learn to listen more carefully to His positive guidance in even the little things and reap amazingly large benefits.

The Lord was speaking to me about catching up on our giving. I agreed to do whatever He enabled. Immediately, guess what He did? He revealed a mistake in our bookkeeping that reduced our tax liability by the amount of the tithe checks I especially wanted to write.

We need to learn to be sensitive to whatever He says to us. In order to develop our sensitivity to Him, we may have to go seemingly overboard. For instance, to not do apparently harmless things forbidden by an over-sensitive conscience is better than to harden our hearts by ignoring that still, small voice. This, too, is applying the cross to our idols. By proceeding with any matter while we're still in doubt, we sin and grieve God's Spirit. We'll never learn to walk as well as we would like in moment by moment loving, open-hearted fellowship with the Lord until we learn to do happily without whatever is doubtful. Our peace, rest, and joy will be limited.

Seek by the grace of God in glad self-sacrifice to do the difficult, the costly, rather than the easy, the naturally desirable that you're doubtful about. Let the Spirit teach you to do it, not to escape God's displeasure or earn God's approval, but to give Him pleasure.

Depend on Him

If you seem unable to release a doubtful thing immediately, tell the Lord so. Confess your incapacity without surprise, remembering the depravity of your sinful heart. Then return to looking in quiet trust and dependence to Him. Look to Him confidently and patiently to cause you to will and to do of His good pleasure. Let Him teach you to depend on Him alone for deliverance.

Years ago I had an experience similar to my TV experience. I'd become enslaved by a very bad habit. One evening when I was engaged in it, the Lord gave me such a sudden revulsion and fear that I wanted to be rid of that habit then and there. I didn't have to promise never to partake in it again as I had done so often. The fear of it, the absolute necessity to be free, said it all. From that day to this, the temptation has got short shrift whenever it appeared, but that was only after years when deliverance seemed unobtainable.

How To Quit Bad Habits

The number of well-meaning Christians who are still enslaved by such habits as smoking tobacco, drinking alcohol, and ingesting other drugs is much larger than many of us recognize. The effect on their spiritual lives is sometimes quite devastating. Once they come to believe the habit to be wrong, it limits their spiritual growth just as does any other cause of a guilty conscience.

We'll never know while here below why God chooses to take such habits away from some people instantaneously, as He did from my father when he received the Lord as His personal Savior, and why, on the other hand, some struggle with these habits for years. Not knowing the answer does not excuse us from dealing with addictions and other sinful habits.

One of my sons-in-law was addicted in his youth. After he received Christ as His Savior, alcohol and drugs dropped off, but the tobacco remained for several years. As we talked about it from time to time and his frustration grew, his question became increasingly, "Should I just wait on the Lord to take it away, or should I decide again I'm going to try to quit?"

Each time he had decided to quit, he ended up returning to smoking and feeling worse than before. At length he became thoroughly convinced that it was harmful and he had to be rid of the habit. He recognized he wasn't able to do it by his own willpower.

He kept pictures of terribly blackened, smoke-damaged lungs in highly visible locations. Then he ordered one of those quit-smoking programs. But by the time it arrived, he scarcely needed it. The Lord had won the day in his heart.

Through the Difficult Delays

Often we need to learn to rest patiently in the Lord while we wait for His deliverance, believing He'll deliver us in His way and time. Such patient trust may be needed concerning our slavery to people and their opinions, to self-will, to passions and appetites, to selfish expectations, and to idolatrous covetousness.

We are morally incapacitated. We simply can't quit! Before His deliverance comes, God must work His changes within. He may need to sicken us of displeasing Him, bring us to the end of any hope in ourselves, and convince us that victory is only in His life. He may sometimes need to do for us what He did for me twice, make us mortally afraid of displeasing Him. In this fear I found, not continuing terror, but the release of mutual love, a rich desire to please my Lord, and the joyful freedom of deliverance.

Don't be satisfied to continue feeding your natural desires. Instead, long for God's enabling to starve them as you have been accustomed to starving your spiritual desires. Let your focus go to Him and to what pleases and glorifies Him. Choose gladly to die to all that feeds or encourages the selfish desires of the flesh.

Let times of uncertainty, weakness, and need be reminders to use the golden key and seek the Lord in peace. Let times of temptation become reminders of your inability to live as those already dead to the world and the flesh. Flee to Him in the secret place of the spirit to receive from Him more desire to will and capacity to do of His good pleasure.

Let God Do It

Whenever you sense that you're rushing, pushing, shoving, impatient, remember that God's children don't have to. Instead they can—they are able to. Slow down, withdraw into your spirit, and recommence your peaceful communion with God in the Spirit. When He's in charge, there's no need for the hurry that's accompanied by tension and anxiety.

Whenever you sense your independence reestablishing itself, reasserting your self-reliance, look to the Lord in rest and peace. Receive His freeing grace. In that grace, die to the claims of the flesh to competence.

Depending on God and not on yourself is reflected in an attitude of simple gratitude that God is right now doing His pleasure without any need of your interference, whether it seems so or not. When we get out of the way, God is most free to work in us. Our anxiety, our necessity, our independence, our hurry, our seeking the credit, our pride, our self-effort, all limit the extent to which God can work His perfect will in our lives and circumstances.

CHAPTER 21

Just Being Receptive

He came to His own,
and His own did not receive Him.
But as many as received Him,
to them He gave the right to become
the children of God,
even to those who believe in His name.
—John 1:11-12

This may seem a strange point at which to introduce this favorite salvation verse. But stick with me, and I think you'll see how beautifully it fits.

God's Way of Personal Salvation

First, what if just one reader has never really received the Lord Jesus Christ as his personal Savior from the guilt and penalty of sin? The God who loves us all sent His sinless Son to die on the awful cross for our eternal salvation. He took our sins and punishment on Himself, making it possible for God to forgive all our sins—even the worst. So we can escape the eternal punishment that otherwise awaits us all as surely as we breathe, and we can live in bliss with Him forever. All we have do is turn from our sin and receive Jesus Christ as our Lord and Savior.

What if you are that one reader? What if you were to miss it all? What if you were to spend eternity in hell? What if it were because I failed to urge on you the need of making absolutely sure you're depending on Jesus alone for your eternal salvation?

No, my friend, that mustn't happen. I owe you that. If you really don't know Him, I urge you to tell Him you've sinned against Him, you deserve His punishment of your sins, and you receive Him as your Savior now. Ask Him to come into your heart and begin the glorious transformation that He alone can make in your life.

To Profess Is Not Necessarily To Possess

Some may wonder if any would have read this far without knowing the Lord and His eternal salvation. Perhaps not, but one of those dear people the Lord has ministered to through me phoned to ask, "What does it mean to be born again?" In her instance, I had no doubt but that she really knew the Savior. She just couldn't stand her imperfection! What better witness could there be that the convicting Spirit lived in her?

However, another instance was different. A husband shared with me his concern about his wife's unresponsiveness to spiritual matters. She'd accepted the Lord at the same time he had years earlier. Now, she didn't even want to go to church. It seemed to be a new idea to him that perhaps she hadn't received the Lord at all and she was just reflecting her unconverted heart by her actions. True, she seemed to grow spiritually in those early days. But had she really been born again? Had she been a spiritual baby growing or were her changed interests just reflecting her husband's changed life and the new church and friends?

Examine your heart, my friend. Be sure you are His. How? Well, perhaps answering these questions as honestly as you can will give you your answer: Do you have any hope other than the Lord Jesus Christ alone for your eternal salvation? Do you think things such as church attendance, trying hard, or being as good as anyone else earn you merit with God? Have you seen yourself as the sinner you are, or do you really think you're kind of a nice person, certainly not a bad one?

There is nothing like a good dose of self-righteousness to keep people out of heaven! The Lord only saves sinners. Do you qualify?

True Stories

My sister, Bernice Callaway, asked our dear maternal grandmother whether she was the Lord's. Grandma replied that she had received the Lord when she was a child. Still, we remained skeptical. She just didn't seem comfortable with the things of God or the people of God.

Quite a number of years later, at the age of 83, Grandma was lying on what she thought was her death bed. There she asked the Lord to be her Savior. In the next ten years before she went home, she listened constantly to Christian radio broadcasts. Her Bible never left her bedside. She really was different.

After having received the Lord at nine years of age, I was plagued by occasional doubts about my salvation for years. If I were really His, wouldn't my life be more pleasing to Him? One day, after I was in full-time Christian service, I was telling someone that, to be sure of our salvation, we need to just cast ourselves on the Lord. We need to stretch ourselves completely out on Christ Jesus as on a hand over a flaming pit, for He is our only hope of being kept out of those flames.

Amazingly, from then on I've never really doubted my salvation. I had accepted Jesus as my only hope and found no need of anything more. My hope had come to rest in Him alone.

Know this: if Jesus doesn't save us, we'll never be saved. We can rest in Him and forget our doubts. Praise His name!

Only the Beginning

We think of John 1:12 as an invitation to a one-time decision to receive Jesus Christ as our Lord and Savior. Truly it is.

But that one-time receiving Christ is also our invitation to constant receiving. With that one-time decision we become children of God, but what do babies do once born? They receive nourishment, protection, warmth, cleansing, love. Without receiving, they could give nothing back, not even the only thing they have to give, the expression of their own need that we see as affection. They'd die.

We're Constantly Receiving

We don't seem to recognize it, but we're constantly receiving from the good hand of God. We couldn't live another instant if we didn't receive life and breath from His sustaining hand. Everything we have or are, we have received from Him, including our abilities to think, to feel, and to choose, our five physical senses, and in a secondary manner all that results from these gifts He has bestowed on us. We couldn't make or acquire anything without the body, mind, and abilities He's given us applied to the material things He's put in this world.

Spiritual Receptivity Is Key

We've described our spiritual life in many different ways. Here's another: a Christianity that really works is one of receptivity to God. If only we knew enough to be just good receivers.

We have nothing to bring to our relationship with God except ourselves in our need. All we have is what He created, and this we've defiled, damaged, and defaced. Even this we wouldn't bring to Him, we couldn't bring to Him, except the Father drew us. So, the only thing we can do in a Christianity that works is be receptive by His enabling to Him.

To receive from God, we don't work. Instead, He draws us in love. With the ability He gives, we respond to His loving drawing. He gives us the gift of faith, and with that faith we trust Him. He shows us we have nowhere else to rely, and only then do we begin to depend on Him. He looks on us with love, and we're drawn to look to Him. He teaches us there is peace nowhere else but in His rest, and we learn to find our rest and peace in Him.

He brings us to see that anything we thought we had is totally inadequate to meet our needs. Only then do we at last begin to come to Him, wait on Him, look to Him, trust Him, depend on Him, rest content in Him, abide and reside in Him, and receive from Him all we need of His all-sufficient mercy, grace, and abundant supply.

We have only to remain in Him, at peace in the place where we were made always to be. At no point does this change, nor should this seem strange. Our Creator designed us this way from the beginning!

Another Way?

What other way could we possibly want than to be forever in the hand of our perfect, all-powerful, loving Father God and Savior, always receiving everything we need from Him? What other way? Pause and think it through. What other way?

You know, don't you? Your way. My way. Our own foolish, self-centered, independent ways. Our destructive ways. Our painful ways. Our ways.

How absurd! How absolutely unbelievable that we should try to depend on ourselves, to seek to be our own supply, we who ultimately have nothing except what our God gives us. How incredible that we should refuse His inexhaustible supply, preferring to try to be our own.

When we do, we're thieves and liars, claiming as our own what came from God's hand in the first place. You see, there's nothing that is that didn't! So we have nothing of our own. Nothing!

Our Foolish Misconception

The world, the flesh, and the devil have misled us into believing that God is in the business of taking away from us, of depriving us. Sure He is! He deprives us of our burden of sin, its guilt, its slavery, and its eternal punishment. God seeks to strip us of all that is harmful, hurtful, and destructive. But He is really in the business of giving to us.

For God so loved the world
that He gave His only begotten Son,
that whoever believes in Him
should not perish but have everlasting life.
—John 3:16

He that spared not His own Son,
but delivered Him up for us all,
how shall He not with Him
also freely give us all things?
—Romans 8:32

God...gives us richly all things to enjoy.
—1 Timothy 6:17

God doesn't deny us anything that is for our good. Rather sin and separation from God deprive us of what is good—our sin and that of our forebearers all the way back to Adam. Yet to that we cling in preference to Him!

In this foolish world, hurting because of sin, God seeks to give us first and most what is most important and most curative. He seeks to give us first Himself in a right relationship—an ever-growing, expanding, loving, fulfilling relationship with Him. This we need more than everything else that we could possibly ask for combined.

"Christ in You, the Hope of Glory"

As Romans 8:32 tells us, with Christ and in Christ, God gives us all things. He in us is our hope of transformation from glory to glory. He is the author and finisher of our faith. We are complete only in Him. Let's look nowhere else. Let's seek to receive nothing so much as more of Him.

Out of Him and His Spirit in us flow life, righteousness, wisdom, sanctification, redemption, love, joy, peace, longsuffering, gentleness, goodness, faith, meekness, temperance, hope, strength, and might. These and so much more flow to us from Him and through us to touch, help, and heal others.

Receptive to Him

By His enabling, let our attitude to Him be one of increasing receptivity in all things. Let us look not to ourselves, but to Him. Let there be in us less and less resistance to Him and what He provides. Whether He is providing love, grace, mercy, compassion, forgiveness, and cleansing, or correction, discipline, and chastening, let us become increasingly receptive to Him. Let us receive His strength and power, not just for the accomplishing of great feats for Him, but even more to enable us to suffer gladly for Him.

I have learned in whatever state I am,
to be content.
I know how to be abased,
and I know how to abound.
Everywhere and in all things I have learned
both to be full and to be hungry,
both to abound and to suffer need.
I can do all things through Christ,
who strengthens me.
—Philippians 4:11-13

Strengthened with all might,
according to His glorious power,
for all patience and long-suffering
with joy.
—Colossians 1:11

Receiving Death to Receive Life

As we take time alone with Him with our hearts open and receptive to all He wants to give us, He'll begin to work an increasing hunger for Himself in us. He'll also develop in us a growing willingness to die to our independent selves so we may live to Him. Primarily occurring during times of devotional prayer, this process also transpires in the quiet of our hearts and spirits alone with Him throughout the day.

We'll find ourselves refusing more of the things held out to us so attractively by the world, the flesh, and the devil. We'll refuse them so we may receive gladly more of what He holds out to us, whether attractive or unattractive to our old man.

To receive of His fullness we must become increasingly willing to let go of all that usurps His place in our hearts and lives. To receive Him initially and His wondrous gift of personal salvation, we had to let go of our sin, prideful independence, and hope in ourselves or in anything other than Him. Just so must we be doing constantly to receive more of Him and His salvation in ever-expanding dimensions in our lives.

But, more than this, we need to let go of our right to control things and people, even to control our own affairs. In short, we need to let Him be in charge.

I'm not, of course, suggesting being irresponsible or uninvolved. But, tell me, what could be assuming greater responsibility than to get out of His way so the One who is infinitely capable can take charge? That is the best kind of responsible involvement. Moreover, we know that the infinitely capable One who is in charge in His infinite wisdom will certainly tell us if, when, and how we should participate in His doing.

CHAPTER 22

Come to Jesus

And the Spirit and the bride say, "Come!"
And let him who hears say, "Come!"
And let him who thirsts come.
And whoever desires,
let him take the water of life freely.
—Revelation 22:17

The way to draw close to the heart of God in a Christianity that really works is simply to come to Jesus. Some of the ways to come are: give Him your attention—focus on Him; worship, love, and adore Him; rest content in Him; abide at home in Him; realize your place in Him and His place in you. In showing you how, I have tried to help you recognize that it's not the human *how* that is important but the divine *Who*. Jesus, as He lives within you, draws you constantly to Himself. You are simply responding to His drawing.

The more you respond to His drawing and come, the better. Come, accepting His word that there is no good thing in you, only in Him. Come, then, with no thought that in the

212

coming there somehow is merit. You may want to respond receptively to Him and His undeserved love and grace, but you can't. Only He that is in you can. Come knowing that the only good thing you can do is respond to His drawing—and this is only by His enabling.

To come with your own goals and purposes in mind, your own plans, and programs is scarcely to come at all. Rather, the ultimate aspiration is to come to Him in such a manner that you might always abide and reside in Him. So, abiding and residing, unresistingly, dependently in Him, you may receive in Him all you need, including your very life.

Why Suffer Unnecessarily?

The retaining of something for ourselves is the cause of our separation from God and the fear, anxiety, and pain that accompany it. We were never intended to be even a thought away from God. We were to reflect Him in all things, to depend on Him for all things, to be apart from Him in nothing, to depend on ourselves and hope in ourselves for nothing.

The anguish occasioned by our separation from God is so needless. In Him is love, joy, peace, longsuffering, gentleness, goodness, faith, meekness, and temperance. Separation from God causes the divisions, the disunity, the conflict, and the confusion that boil in the

213

cauldron of the soul and spill over in anxiety, impatience, fear, envy, jealousy, anger, hatred, and murder. In being reunited to God, in giving everything back to Him, we're made whole.

But how is this accomplished? The answer is in responding to the Lord and finding Him in Himself, not in His truth, nor in an experience of Him, nor in our efforts to please Him.

Always and in all things, come to Jesus. Come to His Father. Come to His Spirit. Come to the triune God. Let everything serve as a reminder to come. Start wherever you can. Let God purify your purposes as time goes on.

When to Come

In need, come to the omnipotent One. In uncertainty, come to the omniscient One. In loneliness, come to the omnipresent One. In failure, come to the infinitely perfect One who is perfectly understanding and caring. In fear, come to the loving Father. In sin, come to the Savior. In restlessness, come to the God of peace. In hopelessness, come to the God of hope. In bitterness, anger, or hatred, come to the God of love. In rebellion, come to the One who died to restore rebel man to his place in God. In sickness of mind, heart, body, or spirit, come to the Great Physician. In pain and distress, come to the Comforter. In need of knowledge, come to the Truth. In need of wisdom, come to Him who is made unto us wisdom. In need of righteousness, come to Him who is made unto us righteousness. In need of holiness of life, come to Him who is made unto us sanctification. In need of redemption, come to the Kinsman Redeemer. In dying, come to the Life. In hunger, come to the Bread of Life. In thirst, come to the Living Water. In need of love, come to Him who is love. In worship, come to the Creator of the universe, the Almighty. In service, come to the One who has all power in heaven and on earth.

In testing and temptation, come to Jesus who was *"in all points tempted as we are, yet without sin"* (Hebrews 4:15). Come to the One who has promised never to allow us to be tempted above that we are able, and who has promised to make a way of escape.

In the uncertainties of daily life, come depending on the infinitely capable God of love. Come to the omnipotent God who is infinitely concerned with the smallest need, or weakness, or incapacity, or distress we may have—and the most mammoth and frightening. Come to the One without whom we can do nothing.

Come Anyway

When you ache from sinful failure and want to hide from God, come to the God who prepared a sacrifice to cover all sin. When you fear to come because your sin is too big or too often repeated, come to the God who has promised never to leave us or forsake us. Come to the One who has promised to be faithful even when we aren't. Come to the One to whom no sin is too great to forgive, no wound too grievous to heal.

When you blame God, come to Him who bore your blame so freely while He was entirely without blame. See your awful antagonism to Him who loves you so. Release it to Him. Receive His love and forgiveness. Begin to revel in His trustworthiness regardless of how things seem to you. When you can't forgive yourself for accusing God, come to the compassionate Father who grieves with your grief.

When you are weary and worn out, come. As you previously ran away from the Lord to a smoke, a bottle, drugs, TV, food, or friends, run to the Lord Himself for your solace. When you can't come, when you're too self-satisfied to come, when you're too lazy to come, when you're too tired to come, when you're too hopeless to come, come anyway to the only source and solution for all your needs, Jesus.

How to Come

Come in need and quiet meekness. Come in trust and openness. Come in receptivity and non-resistance. Come in peace and rest. Come

216

in simplicity and sincerity. Come in freedom —not from compulsion, but from desire. Come in joy that He is always there for you. Come in confidence and expectation. Come in love.

This challenge to come to God always in all things is without worth unless we come in humble, non-resistant, dependent neediness.

Give Him Your Heart

The only sin that will keep you from drawing close to God is an unbroken, unrepentant, unwilling, untrusting, unyielded, independent heart. Whenever you sense yourself being centered on yourself and your wishes, withdraw Godward, and recommence your quiet communion with Him.

Come regardless of how futile or hopeless it may seem. Stay there in quiet confidence that He will Himself draw you in love even if it's unnoticed by you. Trust Him. He has promised He will do it. He has never told a lie.

Only God can draw us to Himself. We need only to allow Him to remove the blockages that we may receive of His grace. By His enabling we willingly respond to His call to die to all that is not Him to live in Him and His joy.

Words would fail us if space did not. Suffice it to say that we can come in everything to the great I AM, who is all-sufficient for us.

CHAPTER 23

Looking to Jesus

Looking unto Jesus,
the author and finisher of our faith.
—Hebrews 12:2

But we all, with unveiled face,
beholding as in a mirror
the glory of the LORD,
are being transformed into the same image
from glory to glory,
just as by the Spirit of the LORD.
—2 Corinthians 3:18

We know that when He is revealed,
we shall be like Him.
For we shall see Him as He is.
—1 John 3:2

Look to Me, and be saved,
all you ends of the earth!
For I am God, and there is no other.
—Isaiah 45:22

One of the myriad questions asked of me by a dear lady living hundreds of miles away was, "How do you look to Jesus?" At the time, I knew her and her husband only by phone and mail. While hooked on drugs, they asked the Lord to send someone to help them. She insisted, "You were His answer to my prayers, so you're my pastor." I rejoice that God allowed me to serve this precious couple and many others in that capacity.

Looking to Him Is Our Hope

The Old Testament expression translated so often in the King James as *"wait on the LORD"* can equally well be *"look to the LORD."* We're told often to look to the Lord throughout the Word. As we study the verses at the beginning of the chapter, we see that it's as we look to the Lord we're changed into His likeness. The passages in 2 Corinthians present this reality most clearly. As you meditate on these Scriptures, let them be a primary motivator in your life, as a reminder to look to Jesus and watch Him change you to be more like Him!

Looking Away from Ourselves

Surely, nothing can be more important than that we look away from ourselves, from our concerns and our idols, from things of time and space to Him. To put it simply, we receive little good, and often great harm, from looking to ourselves. So, any way in which the Lord can turn our attention from ourselves and earthly things to Him is going to be advantageous.

Start receiving the magnificently transforming benefit of seeing Him even a little as He really is. Start in your devotional times. Seek Him by making it your objective to give Him just as much attention as possible, as fully and purely as possible. Let go of your concern for anything that is not Him. Speak with Him. Worship, seek, praise, and thank Him. Reach out to Him with whatever love He gives you. Meditate on Him. Wait quietly, restfully, peacefully on Him. Be willing to receive whatever He gives. Don't try to dictate to Him what happens next. Just let Him guide your sensitive heart in communion with Him.

Certainly, you'll look to Him for your supply of temporal needs of whatever sort they may be. But let them be a distant priority in comparison to the Lord Himself and that which is eternal and spiritual.

Nothing But Him in Your Affections

A real danger exists that we may look to the Lord only with an emotional response that doesn't count the cost of forsaking all to follow

Him. Looking to Jesus is not essentially an activity of the emotions, nor even of the mind or the will. Rather it is primarily a matter of the spirit, which goes beyond mind, emotions, or will so that to think, feel, or decide is not enough. To turn in our spirits from all else, to turn trustingly to Him to receive Him and whatever He wishes to give, that alone is the objective.

The key blockage that must be unstopped is self-pleasing. You must be willing to forsake everything for Him. Let go of all your idols of whatever sort they may be. This means letting go of things external, physical, and temporal and of your worries and concerns. These also may be idols you hold onto that take His place in your view and in your affections.

To the extent you look to your idols of whatever strange sort they may be, to the extent you hold onto them instead of Him, you won't experience the Christianity that really works. All is from Father God through Christ Jesus and the working of the Holy Spirit. However, if you are looking to your pagan idol alternatives, and in effect worshiping them instead of Him, don't expect godly results.

Looking to Him from Our Melancholy

"My heart is filled with disappointment and fear," I wrote to the Lord one morning in my journal. "I hate to confess it, but it's true. The answer is, of course, in looking away from myself, my perpetual disappointment, my failure, my pain to You in quiet trust and confidence. When I look to myself, there is only failure and grief. When I look to You, there is life, and light, and hope! Lord, forgive me for ever looking long at myself.

"What is it for me to look to Jesus? It is to look to my Savior and my God in quiet, unperturbed trust. Yet if I should look to trust and not to You, I find only myself again.

"You are faithful. Here is where we stand or fall—on your faithfulness. If we see in our disappointments Your unfaithfulness, we sink in the mire. If we see in our disappointments our unfaithfulness and, without a pause, look beyond where we feel or see to the truth of Scripture that You are faithful, we find relief, release, and rest. Best of all, if we simply look to You from our first awareness that we are unhappy, look to You, the faithful God, we need scarcely miss a beat."

Only the Jesus of the Book

You need to be sure that you're looking to the Jesus that is, the real Jesus, not a figment of your imagination. The only way to ensure this is to know Him in His Word. Get to know God in all His three persons as He describes

Himself. At the same time, be reminded again, dear one, that your relationship with your lovely Lord is not of the head nearly so much as of the heart and spirit.

Don't seek any easy formula for looking to the Lord. Just go to Him in need, trust, and dependency, in worship and love, in quietness of spirit and peace as often and as fully as possible. As opportunity provides, turn to Him and look to Him throughout the day. Run often into His waiting arms of love. Rest content there with a spirit submissively ready to give up and give over all that is not of Him and with a heart hungry to receive from Him. Abide with Him in peace and receive all the blessings of that abiding.

Yes, looking to Jesus really is the same story over again. But then, it's not magic you need after all, my friend, but a living, practical relationship with your Lord—a Christianity that works!

CHAPTER 24

God Really Can Be Trusted

God is for me.
—Psalm 56:9

I have learned in whatever state I am,
to be content.
—Philippians 4:11

We are seeking loving harmony and unity with God that permit His very life to become ours in actual practice. However, our awful independence still shows itself so often in so many ways, all of them acting as inhibitors to this loving harmony, unity, and flow of divine life that we seek.

Angry with God?

One of the ways we show our awful flesh is displeasure and even anger with God. Now, if you've never really become aware of inner anger against your Maker, the very thought may come as a shock. But, believe me, it's real.

We face pain, illness, financial difficulty, destructive personal relationships, or the loss of a loved one. The Lord permits in our lives circumstances in which we feel uncomfortable, anxious, pressured, fearful, hurt, or deprived. Even the memory of them afterward may be enough to make us angry. While we probably never have thought of it this way, such anger at the circumstances God permits us to endure is actually anger against God.

Obviously, such displeasure with God does not produce harmony and unity with our Lord, but rather separation. Recognized or not, such resentment against God secretly prevents us from yielding our loving, responsive attention to the Lord. We want to run away and hide from Him rather than commune with Him.

Such anger makes us judges of God rather than He of us. Reversing our roles, we have become our own gods. The real God who is our only hope seems untrustworthy, so we're left without hope. After all, who could want to trust an untrustworthy God? Our whole quest to come to God in love is curtailed. Of course, we find no rest or peace, either.

Safely in Charge

One Saturday morning as I lay meditating on the things of God, slowly He began making a precious truth real to me: *God can be trusted!*

I don't need to be afraid of Him or of anything He permits to come into my life. I needn't fear anything at all that might ever come my way. The rest of my life could be lived without anxiety if only I could see Him as He actually is, if I could never lose sight of Him.

God is love, and He loves me. Therefore, He doesn't want anything bad to happen to me.

God is omnipotent. Therefore, He doesn't have to let anything bad happen to me.

After more than forty years as a Christian and thirty years in the ministry, these truths were life-changing revelation to this poor sinner.

He Is in Control

But is He really in control in a sinning world? This question had to be answered if I were to continue believing and acting on this dynamic truth.

After all, God allowed man to sin. He has not yet brought the age of man's rebellion to a close. He's still permitting it to continue. We know this sinful rebellion against God is desperately destructive, disastrous, deadly.

How can He really be in control, when He has apparently allowed sinners to take human will, and life, and circumstances out of His control?

We read His promise:

And we know that all things work together
for good to those who love God,
to those who are the called
according to His purpose.
—Romans 8:28

Yes, we know we should accept anything He says without question, but there seems to be an unavoidable conflict here. The easiest response to this apparent paradox is to ignore the conflict and simply pretend we believe Romans 8:28 to be true. Still, in our heart of hearts we would remain convinced that at best there must be many exceptions and limitations.

That Saturday morning I was in no mood to resist God. He had allowed disaster to strike our lives. Through the circumstances, He had instilled in me a desire to know and experience all the benefits of His truth, whatever that might be. God had brought me to the place of complete dissatisfaction with mere human reasoning. I simply accepted His Word. Still I had to find the answer to this question if I were to continue believing He is always working all things together for my good.

God Has Let Us Limit Him!

Do you have trouble with the idea of man limiting God? Just remember this: God can do anything except go against His own word or character. God chose to leave it to man to respond to His love. He won't force man to respond against his wishes. However, when anyone does respond to His love, the Lord is able to do what He wants for that person's benefit and His own praise, as He promises:

Whoever drinks of the water
that I shall give him will never thirst.
But the water that I shall give him
will become in him a fountain of water
springing up into everlasting life.
—John 4:14

God Is Sovereign

Somehow in His sovereign power, He is able to permit man to go on in his sin, with its attendant harm and hurt, and still keep His commitment to work out everything for the eternal benefit of each one of His children. A mammoth boost to our faith comes from the simple and comprehensive statement in Ephesians 1:11 that He *"works all things according to the counsel of His will."*

Did you get that? God boldly assures us that even in a rebel world, He's working everything out according to His own ultimate purposes. We don't have to understand that or grasp how it's possible. We have only to accept it! Believing it, we can rest content in the assurance that He's in charge of everything, working it all together for our eternal benefit. When we really accept that truth, we have no need to get angry, anxious, frustrated, or bitter about anything He allows to happen to us—no matter how catastrophic it may seem to be.

Excuses Aren't Allowed

That negative, angry responses will be ours on occasion is a fact. But the problem becomes acute when we fail to admit their existence or when we excuse or approve them. Such anger, such resistance toward the Almighty for permitting what we view as unacceptable simply must not be approved or excused.

No matter how justified in human eyes our reactions may seem, no matter how seemingly insignificant, human, or natural they appear, this resistance to God and the circumstances He permits must be recognized and forsaken. Our attitudes must also be seen as they truly are, resistance and anger toward almighty God who permitted those people and circumstances to be in our lives exactly as they are.

Loving Resignation

Seek, as He enables, to sacrifice back in loving submission to Him who gave them to you all the circumstances of your life. Aspire to relinquish them all back to Him with contentment and thanksgiving. Covet nothing other than what He has chosen to send, no matter how distasteful it may seem.

A Better Way

In the years since the Saturday morning God revealed Himself to me as entirely trustworthy, I've been amazed to discover the importance attached to this transforming truth by many of the most godly Christian writers over the centuries. They differ doctrinally on many matters, but they agree that this truth— that we can trust God to work everything together for our benefit—is basic to our relationship with Him.

If we aren't able to trust Father God, what kind of relationship do we have with Him? If we say we can trust Him, but still feel He allows things that are permanently hurtful to happen to us, we're kidding ourselves. That spells disaster to our love relationship with our lovely Lord.

Trust Makes Room for Love

When we know He's in charge, we can see even the seemingly deliberate hurt brought on us by people to be allowed of God for our eternal benefit. Even that visited on us by our brothers and sisters in Christ can be viewed from God's perspective. So we can let God teach us to love those who hurt us, and say what our Lord and Stephen said when dying at their hands. *"Father, forgive them, for they do not know what they do"* (Luke 23:24). *"Lay not this sin to their charge"* (Acts 7:60 KJV).

An Eternal, Spiritual Perspective

We are not able to really believe He's always working all things together for our benefit if we have a perspective limited to time and space! We simply do not have the capacity in and of ourselves.

For example, I break my leg today. Then I lose a $100 bill. Then someone rips into me and leaves me wondering what I did to deserve it. Then you ask me to believe that God has my best interests in mind!

What you are really asking me to do is to discover and develop the longer view—an eternal and spiritual perspective. Then I can see that God may simply be seeking to make me dependent on Him, submissive, humble, and loving. Then I can see that the benefit of those heart attitudes He's developing in me far outweigh the problem of the pain, the loss, and the anguish.

Then God can freely bless and benefit me. Then this blessing and benefit can flow out from me to others, now and eternally. I may even learn someday to say, "If this is the way You can best benefit me and others, and bring praise to Your name, it's alright if You need to do it again Lord. Thank You, Lord."

Only God Can Make That Possible

This response isn't possible for the mere mortal, even given all the facts we have marshalled. So, if you are to have such trust, non-resistance, and love characterize your reaction to seemingly undesirable events, you will need much more than just mental assent to these truths.

The development of this heart attitude requires hours spent alone in God's presence in which He reveals Himself to you as He is. As you do so, He'll change you from the inside out through simple exposure to Himself in His eternity, infinity, omnipotence, omniscience, omnipresence, holiness, righteousness, justice, humility, gentleness, kindness, faithfulness, changelessness, justice, mercy, grace, peace, compassion, and love. During those blessed hours, He will become your life in increasing reality. As His life replaces yours, you will find the fruit of the Spirit growing in you, replacing your ready anger, anxiety, worry, impatience, meanness, unbelief, pride, self-will, and self-striving.

First Things First

My beloved one, don't put off a moment longer letting God and implicit trust in Him begin to become your first priority. This is the God who is always working all things together for your benefit. I pray you will begin to learn to trust Him to bring good to you out of even the worst that can happen.

May He teach you to rest in peaceful reliance on Him, because He is entirely trustworthy. May you come in increasing confidence to know that in His care there can never be a need to be anxious, worried, or fearful.

But if you go on your way ignoring Him—putting your schedule, your desires, and your priorities ahead of Him and His and choosing to depend on yourself rather than on Him—you will never be able to believe He is totally trustworthy. You will never be able to believe He is entirely able to work all things together for your good. You will drastically limit your reception of the good He plans for you.

God will still be working everything for your benefit, but your stubborn heart will have given Him an unnecessary amount to do in your life—work that must be done in effective order from the bottom up. For instance, instead of being able to draw you to Himself in love, He may first have to work on bringing you back from your backsliding. To bring you back, He may have to allow unpleasant things to happen to you. But this, too, is part of working all things together for your good.

He Is Trustworthy

Believe that He can be trusted. Trust Him. Never question what He is doing or why for long. Rest fully in His love. Be preoccupied with His becoming your first priority.

Then, each time you recognize that you are mistrusting Him, look away from the problem to Him in quiet rest, peace, and trust. Whether your mistrust is expressed in anger or anxiety, impatience or fearfulness, self-will or self-striving, look away from the source of the irritation and from yourself. Look away to Jesus. Let all else fade from your vision. Rest in Him. So may you receive more and more of the eternal benefit He is planning for you.

Three Outstanding Benefits

This practice introduces at least three wonderful advantages into our daily walk with the Lord. First, whenever we surrender our circumstances gladly to Him, we find our attention returned to our Lord from wherever it may have wandered.

Second, whenever we gladly accept what He has sent our way, no matter how distasteful it may seem, we are again in the place of submission to the Lord. We are delivered from that reassertion of selfish independence that has such a devastating effect on our quest to walk always in loving harmony and unity with Him who is the very life of our life.

Third, offering the difficult circumstances back to the God who permitted them for our good and His glory encourages the generation of a quietness, rest, and peace, a gentleness and sensitivity, a kindness and compassion, a meekness and humility, a contentedness that we may have felt was not possible for us. This happy non-resistance has a marvelously liberating effect on the whole personality.

Wondrous Results

As resistance and rebellion are replaced by submission and responsiveness to His Spirit, we find the fruit of the Spirit spontaneously being formed within us. Then, wonder of wonders, we watch the overflow of the Lord from our lives into the lives of those around us.

We may be surprised at how some of those around us seem to grow in the Lord when they don't give Him nearly as much time and attention as we do. Could it be that they are benefitting from the overflow from our lives?

CHAPTER 25

The Subject of Failure

For I know that in me (that is, in my flesh)
nothing good dwells;
for to will is present with me,
but how to perform what is good
I do not find.
For the good that I will to do, I do not do;
but the evil I will not to do, that I practice.
...O wretched man that I am!
Who will deliver me
from this body of death?
I thank God—through Jesus Christ our LORD!
—Romans 7:18-19, 24-25

To speak of the victorious, exchanged life as though it were without pain, frustration, and failure is sheer folly. For that perfect state, we must wait for heaven.

The more we long to please the Lord, the more dissatisfied we may tend to be. This may stop us from resting content in Him. Neglecting to adequately recognize and deal with this reality may have helped bring into disrepute much that has gone under the heading of the deeper Christian life to the extent that the teaching has generally fallen into disfavor in the church.

Made for Perfection

How are we to handle disappointment at our failure to experience all God has for us? First, we need to be prepared with the recognition that God created us for perfection. He has recreated us also for perfection by the new birth. Perfection will be ours someday. Then alone will we live without disappointment.

As still-sinning people in a sinning world, we can be happily content with the Lord Himself and with what He is preparing for us. This is entirely different, however, than pretending to be satisfied with our still-sinning selves in a sinning world.

So, how do we handle the disappointment? Simply by running into the arms of Jesus. Or to phrase it another way, to live contentedly complete in Him who is in us our all-sufficient Savior. Remember the failure is not in Him but in us. He is no disappointment. He is, instead, our only hope. There is no alternative to Him.

We're back to chapter one. Only in our failure and disappointment does our hope lie. So it ever shall be until we finally look upon Him as we never have been able to look before. Then, seeing Him fully as He really, perfectly is, we shall be changed into the likeness of His perfection.

To recognize this reality is not to lower God's standard one bit. Let us elevate His perfect standard and with it the recognition that it is only He who can achieve it to any degree at all, even in us. The extent of His achievement in us will correspond to our willingness to let Him empty us of ourselves to fill us with Him.

Less than Satisfactory

At times we suffer from extreme discontentment in spite of improvements in our responsiveness to the Lord and His call on our lives. Because we were made for perfection and nothing less will fully satisfy, and perhaps because of our faulty expectations, we become discouraged with ourselves. We may still be actually expecting ourselves to perform up to our godly desires, forgetting that here we never shall fully do so. We may have forgotten that if any good is found in us at all, it is only Christ and His life in us.

We have our eyes on ourselves rather than on Him who alone is perfect. We must learn to be satisfied with His perfection. We can be gratefully confident and content in Him that He has accepted us in the beloved. He has placed His perfection to our account so we need

238

not live under His condemnation. Since we are
not under His condemnation, then we needn't
be under that of our consciences either.

This is no invitation to a careless response
to our sinful failure. It is to elevate His grace,
and His complete and adequate provision for
all our need. It is to reaffirm our utter and
absolute dependence on Him alone.

Why Our Disappointment?

We may be failing to put our self-pleasing
to death on the cross, which results in our
spirits being grieved, as is His Spirit. There is
no short-cut. We must agree with Him and let
Him apply the cross to our self-pleasing.

Possibly we aren't living in His peace. We
are distraught due to discontent with what He
permits in our lives. So we are responding
negatively to things and people. Perhaps we
are permitting ourselves to be hurried and
harried, always having to do something.

We may be looking for feelings the Lord
doesn't choose to give us just now. We need to
be content with what He does give.

We may be living under entirely unnecessary condemnation. During my Bible school
days, I recall getting up morning after morning
with a guilty feeling. Finally I told the Lord
that if He didn't show me where I was grieving Him, I would have to assume I wasn't

living in any specific, unrepented sin. The guilty feelings left and did not to return.

If the evil one can keep our eyes off the Lord and on our supposed successes or failures, if he can get us living under false condemnation, if he can deprive us of our joy and peace, if he can get us running around hurried and harried, if he can get us discontented, upset with God at our lack of good feelings or at our circumstances, if he can cause us to live in unnecessary discouragement, he will have accomplished a great deal to destroy our growth in the Lord and His love. Beware of the danger that he will use it to finally cause us to stop seeking the Lord in love. God forbid!

Handling Discouragement

To know spiritual truths with our minds is one thing. It is quite another to submit ourselves repeatedly to Him to reproduce those truths in us by His life.

So what can we do when we suffer from failure and disappointment? First, remember that our satisfaction must always be in Him, never in ourselves or our supposed achievements. We find nothing in our independent selves but failure and disappointment.

Second, recognize that God is working all things together for our good. Recognize that He is even using our failure and disappointment to drive us repeatedly to Him. So what seems to be the greatest failure and disappointment may be turned by the grace of God into one of the greatest steps forward. You will have many opportunities to thank God for having allowed you to fall flat on your face so you recognize your folly and hopelessness and cast yourself on Him as your only hope.

Twice in consecutive meetings, I sharply reprimanded someone. After the first incident I apologized. After the second I wrote two letters. One was another apology sent by itself to the individual so there could be no doubt that the apology was clear, complete, and without excuse. The second was given to everyone in the group, repeating the apology and explaining the concerns of my heart before God. Not only did the Lord do me good in humbling me and showing me once more my wicked heart and need of Him, He worked to answer prayers that had been lifted to Him for years.

Third, know that God is always accomplishing His eternal purpose of conforming us to His own image. We don't need to feel it is true, but we must know it is so because He declared it. At times of greatest distress at our supposed failure, if we could see as He sees, we would often see great progress being made.

Fourth, reject despondency as self-pity, another form of self-centeredness. Don't be tricked into believing that grovelling in your failure is evidence of humility, spirituality, or even sincerity.

Fifth, recognize how good and right it is to be disappointed in our independent selves so that we may run more quickly to Him, lean on Him harder, look to Him the more intently, and better appreciate Him in us, us in Him.

Sixth, let it make us hungrier for heaven where we shall see Him as He is and be like Him. There we will bask in the light of His infinite perfection, and share in it forever.

Rejoice Anyway

Rejoice in the LORD always.
Again I will say, rejoice!
...Be anxious for nothing, but in everything
by prayer and supplication with thanksgiving,
let your requests be made known to God.
And the peace of God,
which surpasses all understanding,
will keep your hearts and minds
through Christ Jesus.
—Philippians 4:4, 6-7

Be grateful to God rather than complaining and dissatisfied. Rest in Jesus. Be content in Him and His righteousness placed to your account. Be grateful for the changes He has made and is making—and that He hasn't left us to our own devices.

Humbly accept your imperfections and limitations as permitted by God. In other words be content even to be left grieving over our sin because God has permitted it. Be grateful He loves you enough to cause you to grieve over your sin and sinfulness rather than leaving you content with it. This will leave you with a kind of joyful sadness that is humility, meekness, and brokenness of heart.

In all things bow to Him. Bow in worship that He loves you at all in your sinful state rather than complaining at His leaving you imperfect. Be glad for His perfection that is already yours as His gift in principle, and that someday will be fully yours in actuality.

We can rejoice in Christ Jesus in spite of our failure and sin. He is our victory. We are under His shed blood, dwelling in Him and His righteousness. He alone practically changes defeat into victory, death into life. As we look to Him from ourselves, rejoicing in Him, giving thanks to Him, and committing ourselves to Him, He does His transforming work of conforming us to His image. To worry over our failure is actually to remain centered on ourselves rather than on Him. You already know what failure this secures.

Simply tell Him, "Lord, you can never expect anything better from me. Only from you." Leave it there in His tender care, not casually, carelessly, unconcernedly, or irresponsibly, but in simple abandonment of yourself to Him as your only hope.

Living in Victory?

The only living in victory there is for us is living in Him. He is our victory. At best we'll fail and fall short of perfection. Let's not pretend we live in a constant state of victory or pseudo-perfection. We never shall in this life.

Run often to Him. Rest as fully as possible in Him. Be content in Him. Live in Him and His perfection. He is our victory!

Extra Precautions

When we don't find the perfection in our working Christianity for which we long, what must we be especially careful to avoid? Of course, it's especially that the evil one may use our discouragement to get us to give up our pursuit of the Lord, or at least to keep our eyes off the Lord and on ourselves.

Beyond these, we may be turned into liars and hypocrites, living in pretense. Unwilling to admit our failures and disappointments, we may become spiritual phonies, laying claim to more than we possess. Preachers, Bible teachers, and writers are especially prone to this. We may simply accept such truths as right without ever being taught them by the Spirit, or we may have been Spirit-taught but somewhere along the line stopped responding to His inworking. In either case, we may truly believe that it is God's truth and does really work, but just not satisfactorily for us.

We forget that discouragement over our failure is best calculated by God to drive us to Himself. We forget it is there we may learn to lean on Him like the cripples we are. We forget that only there we may learn that we are without spiritual life or hope of it in our independent selves. We forget that our need drives us to depend on the life of Christ within.

Let's thank the Lord for our neediness. Rejecting any pretense of attainment, let's run rejoicing into His arms of love. Even as we seek to teach others, let's be willing to acknowledge publicly that we, too, are just children sitting at the feet of the Master to be taught of Him.

Required Surgery

Our sin qualifies us for the grace of God in the same way that a tumor qualifies us for the surgeon's knife. In no way does the admission of the existence of the tumor intimate that its presence is approved. To the contrary, the appeal to the surgeon's knife is an admission of the unacceptability of its presence as a threatening and dangerous foreign body. So also our appeal to the grace of God to attack and destroy the sin in our lives acknowledges the unacceptability of sin to us.

Sometimes the tumor must become obvious or even life-threatening before the victim can recognize it and turn to the surgeon for help. Likewise, God sometimes needs to allow the severity of the sin to become clearly destructive before we will turn to Him, our only source of help. We best value the grace of God in the light of the horrible nature of our sin.

Lack of Trust

Why can't we simply trust God in all things? No matter how far along we get, as long as we are still in the body, we will find ourselves responding more or less frequently to trials, troubles, and trauma by mistrusting God, even accusing Him in the deep recesses of our hearts of doing us wrong.

We are afraid. We hurt. We get angry. We can't see the hand of a loving God permitting a particular circumstance for our eternal benefit. So we respond with mistrust that is at its heart calling the God of Romans 8:28 a liar.

At such times, God help us to turn quickly to Him where we will see that it is not He, but we who lie. We have sided with the father of lies against the Father of love. Oh, let us quickly forsake that ground. To say it is treacherous is to vastly understate the truth.

Reducing Formula

What is the secret to decreasing the awful extent of our failure? Our problem is the flesh, the old man, our selves independent from God. These independent selves not only sin and fail, but they pretend both to want spiritual victory and to be able to find their own way to it.

The fact is contrary. While our selves, independent from God, are trying desperately to find what we can do, God has already done all that needs to be done. Jesus did it on the cross. The victory is won.

Still, the flesh insists on trying to win by its own efforts the victory already won for us and given us as the free gift of God's grace. It tries to convince us that our union with Christ is insufficient. It seeks to persuade us to try to fight it with its own tools rather than accept its defeat at the cross as sufficient for us.

Not Trying, But Trusting

Our victory, then, is not by trying but by trusting. It is by resting in Him and in His victory already won.

But that isn't our reaction. In fact, we find it not only incredible that victory is in rest, we find it repugnant. Instead, our first response to each new challenge is to try harder!

As we've already observed, our first response in every circumstance needs to be just to stop, back away from the problem, look to Him, recall our position in Him, relinquish everything into His care, and rest in His victory.

Isaiah 30:7 (KJV) says, *"Their strength is to sit still."* Isaiah 26:3 says the Lord *"will keep him in perfect peace whose mind is stayed on [Him]."* Only in this atmosphere of quiet rest, peace, and trust in the Lord can the Spirit of God produce the fruit and the victory which is distinctively His in our lives.

Oh, how well do I know how hard it is to believe it and simply to yield to Him in rest as our hope. But there is no other way, my friend.

CHAPTER 26

At Home in God

Abide in Me, and I in you.
As the branch cannot bear fruit of itself,
unless it abides in the vine,
neither can you, unless you abide in Me.
I am the vine, you are the branches.
He who abides in Me, and I in him,
bears much fruit;
for without Me you can do nothing.
...These things have I spoken to you,
that My joy might remain in you,
and that your joy might be full.
—John 15:4-5, 11

What does the word *home* suggest to you? Safety, relaxation, rest, peace and quiet, comfort, contentment, acceptance, frankness, unpretentiousness, openness, trust, and warmth are terms that come to mind for me. Home is the center of concern, caring, and love, the kind of place anyone wants to be. There a person finds the encouragement, support, correction, direction, and assistance he needs to keep going through the roughest times.

But there is more than this for us at home in God. He doesn't want just to somehow see us through. He holds out to us something of the delights of a perfect eternity beginning even now in this wicked, sin-sick world.

In Your presence is fullness of joy;
at Your right hand
are pleasures forevermore.
—Psalm 16:11

These things have I spoken to you,
that My joy might remain in you,
and that your joy might be full.
—John 15:11

The word here translated *remain* is the same word translated *abide*. Abiding, or living, or staying, or remaining at home in God is staying at home in joy. What a delightful thought! It's being at home with God in contentment, peace, happiness, and joy.

I want you to keep these images of this kind of restful, joyful home in God in mind as we look at the picture the Lord gave us of abiding in Him.

Not Cold Theology

Remember, what we have here is a picture, not theology, but illustration.

While still a teenager, I read a book on this passage by the most prolific of deeper-life writers. I confess, while I valued its emphasis on walking closely with the Lord, I understood little of it. It seemed far too deep and theological for me. While I appreciate it more now, I still wonder whether the picture the author presents is as down to earth as the Lord intended it to be.

Begin with Trust

Another writer of the same era tries to simplify it by saying that abiding is simply trusting. Abiding in Christ surely begins with trusting God and rests entirely on trust. How could it be otherwise? The whole of our relationship with the Lord begins and rests on trust. If God isn't to be trusted with our well-being, who is? Where is our hope? Surely, then, life must lack stability, a rock on which to anchor, a citadel to which to flee, protection from the storms of life, a firm foundation on which to build.

But as I have tried to impress on you, our God is completely trustworthy. He is entirely willing and able to care for every circumstance of our lives and bring from each eternal benefit for us and others, and glory to His own name.

To abide in the Lord is surely to trust Him. But, helpful as it is, to view abiding in Christ as only trusting Him is incomplete and inadequate. Being at home in God, or abiding in Christ, summarizes all the essential realities I've tried to present throughout this book.

For instance, before we can be at home in Him, believing He is always working all things together for our eternal benefit, He must humble us. Certainly He must do so before He can teach us more—the abundantly above all we can ask or think more that He has for us.

A Prisoner's Problem

For several years, I have been counseling a young male prisoner by phone. When I was first put in touch with him, he thought he had the same intimate relationship with the Lord as the godly folk of centuries gone by whose writings he was reading, only possibly better! In reality, he was always complaining, showing little confidence in the Lord.

After some months, he finally stopped expressing this pretense. But I questioned whether I should continue counseling him because he resisted any direction or correction I offered. His conceit had not changed, only its expression. He wanted his fellow prisoners who professed to know the Lord to look to him for Christian materials and guidance. I wondered whether, by paying attention to him, I was only confirming him in his prideful ways.

Having about given up, one day during a counseling phone call, I found myself asking the Lord to turn the conversation from self-concerns to spiritual topics. Immediately the young man asked me whether I might help him with something. He told me the Lord had withdrawn Himself from him to such an extent that he couldn't even talk to others about the things of God without feeling guilty and hypocritical. How I praised God! Here at last was a glimmer of hope.

Accepting Correction or Affliction

Jesus opened the sermon recorded in John 15 with these words:

> *I am the true vine,*
> *and My Father is the vinedresser.*
> *Every branch in Me*
> *that does not bear fruit He takes away;*
> *and every branch that bears fruit He prunes,*
> *that it may bear more fruit.*
> *—John 15:1-2*

We need to become willing to let the Lord humble us to accept His pruning and purging. We must accept it from Him whether it comes through His servants' instruction, the sandpapering of abrasive fellow-Christians, or the pain and suffering of affliction. Before the fruit of the Spirit can bloom and grow in our lives, we must accept His humbling.

Uncomfortable

Most people live life feeling anything but at home. They live in deep discomfort. They are anxious, fearful, ill at ease, always resenting what life dishes out to them.

Many Christians live feeling anything but at home in God. They share their worldly counterparts' discomfort and fearfulness. But more than this, they feel uncomfortable, condemned, and ill at ease with God and their Christianity. In fact, they are upset most of the time.

Far from knowing the comfort of accepting things as they are at each moment, with gratitude to the God who sent them for their benefit, they live in constant resentment, resistance, and rebellion toward them and toward the God who sent them. They have never been humbled to accept His way as best no matter what it may be.

Of course, they may get very upset with you if you suggest it is so. They are constantly in bondage to negative responses: unkind thoughts, ingratitude, resentment of their circumstances, unforgiveness, frustration, anger, bitterness, anxiety, and fear. The rest and peace of being at home in God is little known or experienced, so they are deprived of the joy that is their right. Far from giving thanks in all things as the Word admonishes, many murmur and complain quite constantly.

Entirely Present

May the Lord teach us to let go repeatedly of all that is not Him or His. It makes no difference if it is our selfish delights or our pain and distress. We must let go of it to Him, or else we will never be set free from our bondage to live peacefully at home in Him.

The branch rests contentedly at ease in the vine. Quietly, calmly, without stress or strain, it receives the life of the vine for its own life and for the production of fruit. Being in Christ and He in us is this quiet receptivity of His life as our own. This is the rest that is the golden secret. This is the loving communion and communication that flows primarily from Him to us, and of which we return just a little.

The Foolish Branch

The branch would be very foolish indeed to look to itself, to depend on itself, to rely on itself, to hope in itself, to count on itself, or to try to draw on itself to receive from itself the life to sustain it and produce fruit. We are just as foolish when we try to find in ourselves the life needed to sustain our spiritual lives and produce spiritual fruit.

Instead we must look only to our Lord. We need to depend on Him, rely on Him, hope in Him, count on Him, draw on Him, receive of Him His life to sustain our spiritual lives and produce spiritual fruit. We need to know that just as the fruit is not the fruit of the branch, but the fruit of the vine, so the spiritual fruit is not ours, but the fruit of the Spirit.

Abiding in Christ is simply resting and remaining receptively in the Lord, being at home in God, letting Him do the work, letting Him get the praise. Let's begin being more fully, constantly at home in Him.

Always at Home?

If we can just rest contentedly at home in Him, living in the dynamic of His life in us, why does there have to be the coming, the turning and returning I have described? Simply because, instead of remaining at rest in our home in God, we wander in self-will and rebellion. We are not content to receive the constant flow of His Life in us. We want to rely on our own resources. Instead of looking in restful trust to receive from our God all we need, we look idolatrously to ourselves or elsewhere.

Why would anyone want to wander from his home in the all-sufficient God where he can be completely at ease, contented in absolute confidence in the love and provision that is always there for him? Irrational as it may be, we do wander in many ways small and large.

Our abiding may never be as constant as we would wish. We may always be tempted to waste our time questioning why. Instead, let us be quick to count on the grace, love, and mercy of the Lord. Upon each recognition of wandering, simply run back into His arms to again rest and remain at home in Him. After all, it is the best place we could possibly be. Tell Him honestly you have foolishly wandered away from Him. Do it without either hesitation or aggravation.

Keep yourselves in the love of God.
—Jude 21

Rest contentedly at home in God and His love. Trust yourself to God and His love. Wait at home in God and His love. Rely on God and His love. Be confident in God and His love. Receive the love of God. Be responsive to the love of God. Be renewed in the love of God. Enjoy the Lord and His love. Remain in His love. Don't separate yourself from Him and His love. Be at home in God and His love.

Does this sound like a lot of work? Realize who is really doing the work, the keeping, as you read the context of the following:

But you, beloved, building yourselves up
on your most holy faith,
praying in the Holy Spirit,
keep yourselves in the love of God,
looking for the mercy of our LORD Jesus
Christ unto eternal life.
...Now to Him who is able
to keep you from stumbling
and to present you faultless
before the presence of His glory
with exceeding joy,
to God, our Savior, who alone is wise,
be glory and majesty, dominion and power,
both now and forever. Amen.
—Jude 20-21, 24-25

CHAPTER 27

God Wants You To Be Happy

Blessed [happy] *are those who hunger
and thirst for righteousness,
for they shall be filled.*
—Matthew 5:6

Recently as I was reading a new book that addressed the topic of the Christ-centered life, I recognized my lack and need once again. Unexpectedly the Lord told me, "Be happy."

In the past, I had been almost afraid of being happy. Erroneously looking at all of life's negative circumstances, I sometimes feared that it was God's duty and responsibility to hurt me. The idea of His wanting to make me happy was quite foreign.

Taught as a child that happiness was of the world and that only inner joy was of the Lord, I found my distorted thinking reinforced in Bible school. There I was instructed that happiness depends on external happenings, but only the joy of the Lord is our right and our strength.

The problem with all that high-sounding spiritual philosophy is that, while we understand happiness, the concept of joy is illusive. Joy somehow seems distant and ethereal, or perhaps too theological. And when anything sounds theological, it seems to many of us also to be unobtainable.

But the joy or happiness of the Lord is our strength. I would like to live today and every day in happiness, wouldn't you?

God's Kind of Happiness

God's happiness is not continual joking and laughing. It is not a constant high or some kind of euphoria. It is not a jovial temperament or a bubbly personality. It isn't even primarily a feeling.

This kind of joy is truth. His joy is the fact of the reality of Christ in me, my all-sufficient supply, and I in Him, where I can rest confidently in Him and His supply. It is the fact of sins forgiven, a clear conscience, of being in God's family, and of being at home in Him.

True happiness is not the emotions, but the reality. Happy feelings may accompany or result from the realities; but if not, the real underlying joy can still be there based on the realities, even without the effervescent feelings.

This joy or happiness is freedom from all kinds of bondages. It is thankfulness, gratitude to God for all His kindnesses, and being well-pleased with what God has provided. A peace of heart that isn't just a transient feeling leads to hope and anticipation of what God has in store for us. The inner contentment, gladness, and delight in the Lord is based on who He really is, not on our changing circumstances or metabolism. The only way we can have this kind of happiness is knowing and living in God.

We live in God, so we live in reality. Christ is in us, our all-sufficiency; we are in Him where we can rest confidently in His victory. This is fact. This is reality. Not only do we live in Him, but also we live under the constantly cleansing and freeing work of His blood. This, too, is fact and reality.

Free from a Condemning Conscience

Now, how do these divine realities practically relate to our freedom from a condemning conscience, and so to the realization of our happiness in the Lord? Can we be happy in spite of our inner depravity and our outer sin, weakness, and failure? How can we look to Him freely and dwell in Him at liberty so long as we are beset by sin? How can we be open and free, content and happy in our relationship with Him while we have an accusing conscience? How can we be free to live at liberty in Him and He in us?

Only through God's intervention by the blood of Christ and our full reliance on His blood sacrifice on our behalf, and through His finished work on the cross and His gracious application of it to our lives, are we *accepted in the Beloved* (Ephesians 1:6). Not through our achievements, our perfection, or our lack of sin and failure, but through the blood of Christ are we *made near* (Ephesians 2:13). By appealing to the efficacy of His own blood sacrifice for us, Christ Jesus, sitting at the right hand of the Father, intercedes for us. Praise God, He can never be denied.

Whenever the accuser of the brethren appears telling us we are not acceptable to our God, we need only point to the blood. In it is the assurance of our acceptance, however unworthy of it we may be in ourselves.

Relying on the Efficacy of the Blood

Our place in Him and He in us, our union with Him that provides the free flow of His life in ours, is made possible by the finished work of Christ on the cross. We reckon His righteousness imputed to us, our death to sin, our union with Him, and His empowering life in us as all freely ours through His shed blood. We count on its efficacy for us and in us.

As we lay ourselves down in Him and His righteousness, we rest contentedly, happily there. We dare do nothing else. Certainly we dare not trust ourselves, for we have no righteousness of our own. We have nothing else to place our trust in except Him.

Looking to the Lord Jesus, we learn to commune intimately with Him and the Father. We do so without undue concern for our nature and acts of sin, recognizing that *"if we walk in the light as He is in the light, we have fellowship with one another, and the blood of Jesus Christ His Son cleanses* [keeps on cleansing] *us from all sin"* (1 John 1:7). This walking in the light that guarantees our fellowship is not walking in some kind of perfection. It is walking in Him who is light. It is walking in confidence in Him and His blood, in our position united with Him, and in His righteousness so freely credited to us.

Why has He provided so amply for us poor sinners? *"That your joy* [happiness] *may be full"* (1 John 1:4) He wants us to be happy! Moreover He has provided fully for it in Himself and His shed blood.

How To Be Happy

God is light,
and in Him is no darkness at all.
If we say that we have fellowship with Him,
and walk in darkness,
we lie, and do not practice the truth.

But if we walk in the light
as He is in the light,
we have fellowship with one another,
and the blood of Jesus Christ His Son
cleanses us from all sin.
If we say that we have no sin,
we deceive ourselves,
and the truth is not in us.
If we confess our sins,
He is faithful and just to forgive us our sins,
and to cleanse us from all unrighteousness.
—1 John 1:5-9

How we revel in His provision of Himself and with Him all the righteousness we need so we can be accepted in the beloved through the blood of His cross. But it is necessary that we both see our awful sinful depravity and recognize our acts of sin in order for the blood to be precious.

In addition to pointing to the blood and abiding under it to be safe from the accuser of the brethren, we need to let it be applied to our ongoing sin. When Peter offered to let the Lord wash him all over, Jesus told him that had already been done at his initial salvation. Now all he needed was to have his feet washed to be free from the contamination of the day.

This describes our need, too. We've been washed in His blood, redeemed, and made new. More than that, as we walk in Him and His light, the blood just keeps on washing away the sins of which we are unaware.

The Spirit also reveals specific sins to us so that we might willingly confess and forsake them. Any living with known but unconfessed sin leaves that area of our lives uncleansed. Let us be careful to walk in the light of His truth, quickly confessing our sins to God, and when appropriate, to men. Let's be ready to make restitution where that is indicated, and walk on with God and men with an open heart and countenance. Nothing less will allow us to be really happy.

Living in Reality

Any living in the darkness of falsity and pretense denies the necessity of the cleansing of the blood through which we are *"made near."* It denies us real freedom and happiness. But Jesus told us, *"You shall know the truth, and the truth shall make you free"* (John 8:32).

To live in darkness is to live in sin, but also it is to live in any untruth, any unreality, any pretense, anything other than that which actually is. To live in unreality is to live in slavery to a make-believe world that doesn't exist. That kind of insanity is only made possible by sin.

Of course, it's bound to result in unhappiness. If we would be content, happy, and free in Him, there can be no pretense, no self-defense, no hiding from the unattractive truth. We need to agree with God about our position in Him and His righteousness under the blood, as we do about everything else.

In reality, our wondrously free and gloriously dynamic position in Him and under His blood is our entrance to happiness in Him. Our happiness isn't in a giddy fantasy that all is well with the world. Rather, it is in Him alone and His provision for us in our sin and need.

We need freely to acknowledge both the utter depravity of the old man and our acts of sin, carelessness, lovelessness, selfishness, and failure. We need to remember these things spawned our unhappiness in the first place, and that they grieve God's loving heart.

Though we don't deserve it, He draws us in love as only He can. As we look to Him in response to His drawing, He reveals ourselves in all our sin and sinfulness. At the same time He reveals Himself both in His ample supply, and in His attractiveness, preciousness, wonder, love, and trustworthiness, too. His Father-love is at the heart of everything He permits in our lives. This wonderful assurance makes it possible for us to trust Him and be happy in a sinning, hurting world.

Our position in Him, under the blood, accepted in the beloved, is the basis of all happiness. Live contentedly in this wonderfully complete relationship with Him. Trust His love and power working every circumstance of your life together for your eternal good. Gladly confess and forsake your sins as He reveals them to you. Rest in your place in Him, His powerful presence in you. Live happily in Him.

Something More

We need to learn to hear His voice and follow it. This reality cannot be escaped, as much as we might wish to do so. Until we long so much to please Him that we want to do what He wants us to do without hesitation, we are simply not going to be as happy, content, and free as we can be. No cost should seem to us too great if only it gives our great and loving God pleasure. Rather it should seem a rich and rare privilege.

We will never achieve this position, or any other place, perfectly in this life. But to get closer to wanting only to please Him, we need to let Him convince us in our heart of hearts that pleasing Him not only makes Him happy, it ultimately is the only thing that will make us happy and free. Let Him teach you to value a clear conscience, His approval, and His pleasure more than all the seductive entice-ments the world, the flesh, and the devil can offer.

A Nagging Conscience

*Happy is he who does not condemn himself
in what he approves.
But he who doubts is condemned if he eats,
because he does not eat from faith:
for whatever is not from faith is sin.*
—Romans 14:22-23

*For if our heart condemns us,
God is greater than our heart,
and knows all things.
Beloved, if our heart does not condemn us,
we have confidence toward God.*
—1 John 3:20-21

We have already discussed the need of listening to the dictates of our conscience. But a part of the divine reality is that we are still depraved sinners in spite of our redemption. So, we do offend the Spirit and our consciences.

Then, too, there is the reality that sometimes we have feelings of guilt we do not need to have. If these problems are not dealt with, the ability to live contentedly in the Lord will be seriously impaired. At the same time, we must not deal with them in self-dependence or they will become a source of bondage, causing rest, peace, and contentment to flee.

A dear lady phoned me to get my approval for not having private devotions the days she worked twelve-hour shifts! She knew better, but she still felt guilty. And God stooped to meet her in her folly through the assurances of this poor servant.

Sometimes God is extra kind. I thought of taking my wife, daughter, and grand-daughter to lunch. My conscience nagged that I probably shouldn't spend the time or money. Just then I opened an envelope that contained a $25 check with a note which read simply: "Isn't it time for a breather, even if it's only a lunch out together for you and your wife—with the enclosed." We had a ball together at the cafeteria restaurant right above Niagara Falls. That love gift covered all the costs!

My thank-you note telling her the story arrived just in time to show her the Lord again and lift her out of discouragement. She wrote back to tell me how God had unexpectedly intervened to ask her to send me that $25.

He doesn't always work so dramatically to relieve us of excessive conscientiousness or unnecessary unhappiness. Still, I thank Him that He knows all things, is greater than them all, and yet cares about every part of our lives.

He Knows Where I Am

God is greater than our heart,
and knows all things.
—1 John 3:20

God knows not just my lack of conformity to His perfection and my uncertainty and self-condemnation, but also that I live under His blood, united to Him in fellowship and love, despite all my imperfections. He knows that His grace alone first gave me acceptance, a right standing with Him. He knows that it will be ever and always His grace alone that will give me right standing with Him into eternity.

In this assurance I can live in happiness and contentment in Him, without being the least content with my imperfections. I can live at peace without being pretentious about my supposed achievements or defensive about my sins and failures. All I need do is abide in Him who is my sanctification as He is my redemption, righteousness, and wisdom.

CHAPTER 28

Back to Basics

We are the circumcision,
who worship God in the Spirit,
rejoice in Christ Jesus,
and have no confidence in the flesh.
—Philippians 3:3

For you readers who desire a condensed version of this book and for you who diligently, prayerfully have been reading every page, here is a summary of key aspects of a Christianity that really works. We begin at the beginning, the starting point which is the basis for all the other principles which follow.

Devote the Rest of Your Life to Seeking God!

That He draws us is true. Without His drawing, there could be no genuine seeking on our part. We simply do not have it in us! Still, no less true is the fact that we need to consciously seek the Lord as fully as He enables us in every way He enables every day of the

271

rest of our lives, regardless of distractions and disappointments.

The wonderful verse with which we began this chapter tells us how to walk with Him in a Christianity that really works. It seems to me to divide our seeking into three simple elements: first, worshiping God, seeking Him for Himself alone, rather than for any thing; second, living contentedly in Him in receptive rest, peace, and freedom; and third, dying to our independent selves, letting go of everything but Him. Into these three elements, all those that follow merge.

Christianity Is a Relationship

Our whole pursuit is to know God as the Person He really is in a personal relationship of growing harmony and intimacy. To do it we must shed our religiosity, our pretense, and our faulty views of God and what He is like. We must begin to see Him in His beauty, glory, might, wonder, kindness, love, holiness, infinite perfection, and absolute trustworthiness. He must become the center and focus of our lives.

Spend Much Time Alone With the Lord

Without this little hope of getting to know Him exists. Make it first priority. Worship Him. Adore Him. Love Him. Seek Him for

Himself alone. Let go of everything to Him. Learn to be entirely open and honest with Him. Listen to His Spirit's prompting. Confess and forsake your sins. Know that no price is too great for the privilege of knowing Him in loving intimacy and bringing Him pleasure and praise. Relinquish everything into His loving care. Let Him give you His quietness, peace, tenderness of heart, rest, and contentment.

Commune with the Lord

Make it your goal to ever more fully commune with Him, worship Him, confess your sin and need. Whether in word, thought, or silently looking to Him, whether at home, on the road, or in your usual or extended times alone with Him, give Him your loving attention.

Don't push yourself. Let it be a restful response to the Lord. Be less concerned with what you do or say in prayer than with what He does or says. Trust His doing, saying, or silence. Be relaxedly at home with Him.

Be Emptied

Alone with Him, let Him empty you of your independent self. Look to Him until He brings you to the end of your rebellion, resistance, and resentment. Let Him break your heart that you would dare want to be independent from your

Creator and God. Let your independence end, your dependence on Him be renewed. Let tears come if they will. Gladly accept the broken heart and transformed spirit and attitude He gives. Seek to carry it gently into the day.

Ask God to Make You Humble, Needy, and Dependent on Him Alone

Don't expect these heart attitudes to come quickly and easily. Recognize that they are opposite to attitudes you've maintained all your life, the opposite of your fleshly human nature. You'll spend the rest of your time on earth seeing them emerge, as God's grace works in you. Allow the Lord to teach you to be grateful to Him for all He deprives you of, and all the discomfort He sends your way to humble you and make you needy and dependent.

God Desires to Work in Your Life

God is far more eager to reveal Himself to you, to commune with you, and to transform you into His image than you ever could be to have Him do it.

In your quiet times commune with Him in tender-hearted receptivity more than seeking Him in excessive striving. Be less concerned to do than to let Him do. Let God be God in directing your devotional praying after His own pattern from moment to moment and day to day. Also, don't judge the success of your prayer times on the feelings generated.

Acknowledge Your Proper Place of Submission

If you have never placed yourself in an over-all position of willing submission and surrender to almighty God, your pursuit of the God of love will be a farce. However far you are from it now, you need to allow the Lord to bring you to that place of submission. However stubbornly resistant to Him your flesh may still be, you will know that to agree with Him in everything is your only proper stance. Tell Him now that, however poorly you may want to have and maintain this attitude, you really do need Him to work it in you.

Repeatedly Turn from Unacceptable, Destructive Responses

The Word shows negative reactions to be works of the old man, the flesh, the ungodly, independent self. Responses of bitterness, anger, hatred, strife, envy, jealousy, anxiety, and fear to people and our environment are unacceptable. They reveal our lack of trust in God to take care of us and displace the fruit of

the Spirit in our lives. God asks that we turn
our backs on them:

Let all bitterness, wrath, anger,
clamor, and evil speaking
be put away from you, with all malice.
And be kind to one another,
tenderhearted, forgiving one another,
just as God in Christ forgave you.
—Ephesians 4:31-32

Whenever tempted to give way to such
behaviors, recognize them as destructive and
sinful. In your spirit turn to the Lord. Seek
quickly to let Him turn you from resistance to
non-resistance, from discontent with Him and
your circumstances to contentedness, peace,
and rest in Him. Let Him have control. Allow
Him to replace your negative response with the
corresponding fruit of the Spirit.

However, we must not pretend we don't
have such negative responses, or that we will
always be able to avoid them. We are not to
deny our emotions, but rather to face them for
what they are. We are responsible to quit
justifying the negative and hurtful behaviors
the Word condemns as though they were acceptable. Then we can confess and forsake our
harboring of them as the sin it really is. We
can be delivered from the curse of being in
subjection to them. We may not be able always

to avert the first surge of such harmful reactions, but we can disapprove them and seek God's empowering to turn from them.

Give No Place to Pretense

God is the all-pervasive Reality and Truth. He cannot stomach any lie or pretense. Nothing is more destructive of our relationship with the Lord than pretense or unreality. So let your heart long for Him to reveal your true self and expose all dishonesty, cover-up, and pretense. Seek His enabling to turn from it as quickly and fully as He makes possible.

Without Him You Can Do Nothing

If something has any value at all, God originated and empowered it. If He didn't, it doesn't. Do not be deceived for a second. Seek His enabling to live in this truth.

Live at Home in Him and His Love

Live as God enables in the consciousness that He is your loving Papa God, always on the lookout for your welfare. This frees you to live at home in Him, trust Him, rejoice in Him, worship, honor, praise, and thank Him.

Cast yourself on Him in every time of need. Reckon on the reality that as you are in Him, so He is in you. Let His all-sufficient life flow freely in yours as you trustingly rely on Him to freely provide everything you need.

When your life is in His charge, you need not be perturbed or anxious. He is caring for all your concerns, providing His own life to meet all the needs of your life and being, so that you may always live content in Him, His rest and peace, without fear and anxiety. Seek His quiet confidence that He is in control of all your circumstances, working them together for your good and His glory.

We may well doubt our love for Him, but we can never doubt His love for us. It is in His love and tender care that we live and move and have our being. Only in full assurance of His love do we have hope, peace, and joy.

Repeatedly Return to the Place of Sensitivity of Heart to Him

Return to the chapel of your spirit whenever you find yourself malcontent, restless, stressful, or striving. Return in times of distress or temptation to where the Lord resides and reigns in peace. Relinquish your troubles and needs to Him, as well as your entire life! Accept the peace you find there as His gift of love to you. Seek to live in Him in peaceful non-resistance, not in self-striving. Recognize contentment or peace in the Lord as the monitor of your responsiveness to Him.

Know the Awful Depravity of Your Heart

Until we know the deceitful treachery that lies in the heart even of the redeemed soul, we'll continue to be unnecessarily victimized by our flesh, our selves independent of God. Invite the Lord to remove your mask and show you yourself as you really are so you no longer need to pretend or defend. Acknowledging our sin, guilt, failure and need goes a long way toward spiritual release, help, and health.

This will require confession and restitution to men occasionally, as well as repentance toward God, but it must be in recognition of our constant certain failure apart from Him, His mercy, and His transforming power.

Admit Your Spiritual Idolatry

Anything that is dearer to your heart than is the Lord is an idol. Your love for it is spiritual adultery. These idols need to be put to the cross and gladly forsaken for Jesus' sake. Long-entrenched habits may sometimes require the special grace of God for deliverance. Start out by admitting your sinful bondage. Let Him teach you that you don't have the power to deliver yourself. Give Him freedom to use whatever means He will to effect deliverance. Wait in quiet contentment in Him. Peacefully at rest, trust Him to work in your heart the changes necessary to enable you to please Him.

Learn Right Obedience Motives

Obey God because of the desire He works within to please Him, not out of the law's demand. As we mature, there should come times by His grace that we long to die to all that self prefers over God and His perfect will, just that we may give Him pleasure.

God Is Everything

He is the alpha and omega, the beginning and the end. Your objective is to be united with Him in purpose and love, dependent on Him for everything, independent of Him in nothing. Your great purpose is to praise, honor, and glorify Him alone, to give Him pleasure.

Elevate Him in your heart to the glorious place of total lordship in your life. Become enamored of your God to the extent that no other goal is worthy of your best attention, time, and concern. Let Him be your great life-interest. He should be the major concern of your daily times alone with Him and increasingly of your every thought.

No failure to achieve this objective must be allowed to deter you from continuing to seek always to keep Him as your life center.

Know the Lord to Be Absolutely Trustworthy

He has nothing ever in mind except your best good for all eternity. To think anything less of Him is to malign Him and mistrust His Word in Romans 8:28. We can depend on His loving omnipotence—and on nothing else.

Not finding Him trustworthy incapacitates you for any other spiritual response. Without trust in Him, your love, worship, praise, and thanksgiving will be insincere and just empty words.

Learn to Worship, Praise, and Thank Him

A heart that sings praises, worships, and gives thanks to our loving heavenly Father and almighty God in all things would be a heart to which all things are possible. However, any attempt to work this up is doomed to failure. We come to Him, and come again, and keep on coming, simply seeking only Him. As we do, we find Him giving us a thankful heart and every other good thing. Until He works this holy work within, let's endeavor to be content with whatever He sends us.

Accept Suffering and Distress as Gifts from God

Father love allows all the difficulties of life to come your way. They are designed as His cutting tools to release you from the things of the world and the flesh, and from the captivity of Satan into God's eternal love.

Let Contentment Rule

In our hearts we have a direction, an inclination toward God or away from Him. We can be content in Christ or malcontent in ourselves. When we resist or resent anything, we turn our hearts away from God by rejecting His providential will for us. We must allow the Lord to teach us more and more not to resist nor resent anything He sends us, nor fear anything He might send us. We must, at the peril of our walk with Him, be content with anything and everything He permits to come into our lives.

To do otherwise is to turn our backs to Him and not our faces. When we rush, we run ahead of Him, and our backs are to Him, not our faces. We mistrust Him and His will in the timing, His competence to see that everything that should be done can be done in peace. This destroys not only the peace and the rest of heart, the contentment, but also the freedom and joy. To live on the positive side of this line with our faces to Jesus is to abide in Christ.

Know Your Position in Christ

Our position in Him and He in us gives us hope. In confident dependence on Him, abide, reside, and rest yourself in Him as constantly as possible. Abide in His righteousness, under His blood, in His life, at home in Him. There receive all He has for you of life and hope.

Be Quick to Be Wrong

Tremendous health, help, and healing is found in readily admitting to God and man when you are wrong. Confess it equally readily to both without pretense or defense. Some leave a trail of trouble behind them just because they have never learned to admit they were wrong.

Seek To Act in Accord with Your Conscience

Enlightened by the Word and the Spirit, your conscience is a gift from God. To act against it is self-destructive. However, for our old selves independent of God to try to live up to the demands of our consciences may be almost equally self-destructive, leading to failure, bitterness, and bondage. Again, let the Lord be your guide, teacher, and provider. Be patient with your own stupid stubbornness. Seek not so much to chop off its evidences as to live in loving harmony and unity with Him who is victor over all.

God's Principles Oppose the World's

Do not expect to live in harmony with this world or its principles. Expect to have to undergo a complete overhaul of your way of thinking, feeling, and responding.

Gladly Die to Self

Let God enable you to be willing to die to your independent desires so you can be free to live in Him and His will. In His love for us, God will do nothing to strengthen our carnal flesh, even when our motives for our actions seem good and right. The best we can hope for is to be cast more on our God. In our weakness is His strength. In our death is His life made experientially real in its work in us.

We died with Him at the cross to any right to any kind of independence from Him. Let us give Him and His loving, living presence in us the preeminence in our thoughts as in our lives. To dwell on our assertions of independence, even disapprovingly, may give them room they do not deserve. To think and look to Him with a loving heart is always to profit.

Guard Your Mind

Feed the spirit. Starve the flesh. Especially guard the eyegate and eargate to the soul. This is more crucial than we give credence. We may say on the one hand we are giving God our heart's attention and affection and seeking to live in constant communion with Him. But if, on the other, we give unnecessary attention to the distractions of TV, radio, or the newspaper for instance, we are deceiving ourselves.

We are robbing ourselves of the fellowship, peace, and joy the Lord wants to give us. We are missing out on much that He would give us, teach us, and show us that may be far more important than we dream.

Forgive

You dare not hold anything against anyone. So long as you do, you will not be fully able to believe God has forgiven and delivered you. Start out by recognizing that you cannot forgive—not really. As every other good thing, the ability to genuinely forgive our enemies is only the Lord's.

Let everything go to Him including all your rights and all your defenses. Let Him work the fruit of the Spirit in you, including love for the unlovely and unlovable. You dare not pretend that those who aren't good, or respectable, or lovable are so. See them as they are in all their ugliness. Then remember that the Lord loved you and forgave you fully and freely when there was nothing lovable about you, when you were still in rebellion against Him. Accept His love, that love He has for you, as enough for them, too.

Know That Only God Can Do the Work

I may suggest things that you can do to find a Christianity that really works. But, in reality, it is He alone who instructs, initiates, and empowers anything that is of spiritual benefit. To try to do anything without coming to Him, looking to Him, depending on Him, resting in Him, or receiving of Him is to turn that supposedly beneficial activity into emptiness, vanity, frustration, and futility.

In fact, there is no Christianity that works. God alone works. In all things it's not so much what we do as what we let Him do.

CHAPTER 29

Warning Flags

*Beware lest anyone cheat you
through philosophy and empty deceit,
according to the tradition of men,
according to the basic principles of the world
[world order], and not according to Christ.
For in Him dwells
all the fullness of the Godhead bodily
And you are complete in Him,
who is the head of all principality and power.*
—Colossians 2:8-10

The previous chapter was a summary of some of the responses to the Lord that He may use to draw us to Himself in love. This is a summary of the dangers that, if not guarded against, may hinder His drawing us to Himself or may cause us to slide away from Him.

My greatest fear for every child of God who starts down the long road of seeking to know the Lord in the intimacy of love is that something might thwart or impede him. Renew your vow to seek all your life to make Him your one object and passion. Do it often. Let nothing deter you, not even the sometimes seeming hopelessness of your seeking.

Block the Blockages to Spending Time Alone with the Lord

You may feel all your devotional time and energy is being wasted. You may think you are going backward, away from the Lord. You may seem to be overcome by sin, failure, and weakness. You may know there is no use.

Don't believe these lies of the devil. Believe the Lord's promise: *"You will seek Me and find Me when you search for Me with all your heart"* (Jeremiah 29:13). He never yet told a lie! So never quit giving Him your time and heart's attention. Let it grow.

Don't Be Misled by Men

Every Christian leader who fails to point people primarily to the Lord Himself is to that extent a false teacher. Some, claiming the Word of God for their authority, point people to some substitute. Many lift isolated passages from their entire biblical context and give them inaccurate meanings. Others simply know nothing of the depths of Jesus Christ. Much of their teaching is a form of religious humanism. Be careful, certainly, not to let your pride mislead you to set yourself up against your

teachers. But in this day too many of t
Lord's people are being misled by shallov
carnal, or heretical leaders.

Don't Let Anything Replace the Authority of the Word

Constantly search the Scriptures to see
"whether these things are so" (Acts 17:11).
Submit everything to the Word. Heed the
direction and correction found there.

Don't Let Anything Substitute for the Triune God

Nothing in your affections, attention,
thoughts, or doctrine should be allowed to
usurp God's place in your life—not any desire
of the flesh, not anything of the world, no
possession, no hope, no religious concept,
nothing else. The greatest, most constant
danger is that we'll not put God first and keep
Him first.

Don't Make the Christian Life Complex

In fact, the Christian life is the essence of
simplicity. Sin has given us such a frustrating-
ly complex world, full of so many unanswerable
questions. God is infinite and eternal, without
limitation except the moral limitations imposed

nfinite perfection. But He is not the author
:onfusion. He is the essence of simplicity and
is His truth. Only our unwillingness to fully
eceive Him with His truth in our hearts and
spirits breeds the frustrating confusion that
overwhelms us with such complexity.

Get to the heart of God. In peace accept
the simplicity that is in Christ" (2 Corinthians
11:3). With Him and His simplicity at the heart
of everything you think, say, and do, find the
confusion subside and His peace reign within.

Never Consider Yourself Beyond Any Sin or Failure

Be always on your guard. Even after the
most wonderful time of prayer communion with
your Lord, you may be lifted up in self-confi-
dence that you mistake for the joy of the Lord.
The evil one may come in to devour and destroy right at that point.

Don't Be Devastated by Your Sin

Don't, no matter how awful it may be.
Worse than the sin itself is your prideful unwillingness to face the Lord, humbly agreeing
with His painful assessment of your failure as
sin against Him. Just acknowledge that any
moment you aren't living content in Him, you
are to that extent living in sinful failure.

Ask for His mercy. Thank Him for it. Ask Him for grace to live at rest in Him.

Don't Be Confused about Who Is Working

Our work is, after all, only our response to His work. As our response to His work, it's only an extension and continuation of His working. Let us view it as such, and give Him the credit.

Let us mourn when we prevent His working from achieving its goals in us by our failure to respond receptively to it. From failure, learn to lean more heavily and trustingly on Him.

Don't Resent Suffering

Accept sacrifice and suffering as from the hand of your loving Father God, who is working every bit of it together for your good. Accepting it is essential to permitting God to draw you to Himself. Guard against allowing a root of bitterness to develop in your heart.

Don't Expect an Easy Life

Circumstances may get easier. But chances are they'll seem externally to get more difficult. The Word is full of the sacrifice and suffering of the Christian life. When writing on the subject of suffering, I was amazed at the number of passages that emphasize the place of sacrifice and suffering in the Christian life, and their value in Christian development.

Don't Live to Please Men

You are to look to God, not to men. Look to the Lord for everything. He is your righteousness, your wisdom, your redemption, your sanctification, your life, your light, your hope, your peace, your way, your truth. He is your... Well, you fill in the rest.

Seek to please Him only. Then, without being at all callous of others' feelings, let the chips fall where they may. You'll wonder at the number of times that, even to your short-sighted gaze, they fall where they should to the eternal blessing of all concerned.

Don't Let Yourself Be Deprived of Your Rest and Peace in the Lord

If anything seems difficult to maintain, it's rest in the Lord, peace, and meekness and quietness of spirit. We are accustomed to living hurried, harried lives. We are unused to really believing that God is in charge of everything for our good. We're naturally anxious, worried, fearful. We don't find it easy to trust the Lord with and for everything. We just can't let go of

the have-to's of life. We want to maintai.
control rather than let Him be in charge.

Regardless of the reason for your loss of
peace, pause. Turn inward, away from everything else to Him. There rest quietly in your
spirit with Him. Lay yourself quietly, safely
down in His arms. Accept His comfort and
protection. Let go of everything into His capable hands and caring heart. Do it often.

If you cannot find His peace without getting physically alone with Him, do that as soon
and often as possible. Use the washroom if you
have no better place, but do it.

Accept His love. It is yours. Live content in
Him and His love. The idea that I really can
live in quiet contentment in Him in a world of
such sinfulness and insecurity has become a
great boon to this striving, struggling sinner.
How I thank Him and give Him praise!

Accept No Substitute for the Overflow of Love

As God fills us to overflowing with Himself,
that overflow will bring blessing and help to
those around us. This results in Christians'
lives being changed as they, too, are drawn to
the Lord. Eventually it will result in those who
do not know the Lord coming to Him. Be willing to be His vessel, empty for His filling,

repared that from you He may flow into other
ives.

Don't Allow Yourself to Blame or
Question God

The basis of your relationship with anyone
is trust. So it is with your relationship with
God. To question why is very often to subtly
question God's motives. Your God is absolutely
trustworthy, so yield to His will rather than
question it.

Don't Assume All Praise Is Necessarily
True Worship

Public praise may be mostly the noisy
excitement of the flesh. Private praise may be
terribly self-centered. True worship focuses on
the Lord in all His majesty, beauty, and infinite perfection. The thanksgiving of a grateful
heart is simply the expression of gratitude for
the God you trust and appreciate. It terminates
the murmuring and complaining that blame
God for our temporary discomfort.

Don't Fall Prey to "Preacher's Pride"

As surely as you develop a desire to walk
more closely with the Lord, the flesh will erupt
in preaching. Often the preaching will be full of

condemnation of everything and everyone else. You will cause offense that is entirely unnecessary and never to be confused with *"the offense of the cross"* (Galatians 5:11). The offense of the cross is occasioned by its affront to sin. The offense of this prideful preaching is occasioned by its own sin of self-conceit.

This preaching is not the overflow of love, but of pride. Ask the Lord to show this to you and teach you to silence it. Ask Him to teach you the stillness of meekness, gentleness, humility, contentment and peace.

Don't Fail to Discern Works of the Flesh

The flesh can think on the Lord, even meditate on Him, or say words of love to Him. But, while it may make a pretense of it, it cannot genuinely look to Him or love Him. Only the Spirit can work that within. The redeemed, new man of the spirit knows the difference.

Let's make it our priority every day to look to the Lord in all the ways the Spirit will teach us, beginning in the daily quiet time. Let's make it our practice as often as possible to stay there in rest until His quietness, rest, and peace come into our spirits, whether this takes a minute or hours. If we must prematurely leave, let us return there as soon and as often as we can. Should any feeling of peace refuse to come, rest that, too, with the Lord, and remain content in Him, feelings notwithstanding.

Be Careful of Going to Extremes

The only extreme in which we can never go too far is in our responsiveness to the working of almighty God in our lives. We can never love Him, seek Him, look to Him, come to Him, trust Him, or please Him too much. In anything else we must be careful of extremes. Nothing is lop-sided about our God. We should not approve of anything lopsided about us.

Listen to Him. Let Him reveal to us the balance that reflects His infinite perfection.

Never, Never, Never Give Up

Hang in there. The God whom you seek loves you and has promised He can be found by you. In actuality, He is seeking you, drawing you, holding you, loving you. When you stop your supposed methods of trying to reach Him, you will discover Him right where He found you.

CHAPTER 30

A System of Checks and Balances

I will cry out to God Most High,
to God who performs all things for me.
—Psalm 57:2

The question is often asked whether there is a serious danger in placing all the responsibility on God for the living of the Christian life. Yes, there certainly is.

We have a great responsibility. We are to hear His call, come and look to Him, seek and worship Him, rest and remain in Him, content to have Him work in us the desire and the capacity to receive all He has to give us and allow Him to take from us all that hurts and destroys. Out of this grows the heart desire to please, obey, honor, and serve Him.

He both initiates and empowers the spiritual operations of the Christian life. But whether we hear Him, come to Him, and receive of Him still remains with us. We are also accountable for whether we will seek to please and obey, honor and serve Him.

However, to try to hear, come, receive, or obey in the energy of the flesh is self-defeating, just as any other fleshly response. We can truly respond only in the trust and faith given us by God. In this sense, all is of Him.

Any action of spiritual and eternal value that seems to be ours is simply the result or continuation of His action in us. Thus, it is more truly His action than it is ours. Unless and until we see it this way, we are stealing the credit that belongs to God.

To learn to rest in Christ's finished work for us and the Spirit's continuing work in us is a life-long process. We certainly don't begin there. So, if the choice is between carelessness about the things of God and self-centered works, some of us may need to err on the side of works for a time. In God's grace, He may use even this to bring us finally to see the futility of our works and come to rest in His finished work and present working.

Self-discipline and Self-denial

I have just been challenged by a book on the place of discipline in the Christian life. I could respond well to it because it started out, as most do not, emphasizing the priority of our personal relationship with God and the necessity of giving Him our attention.

If this approach to living the Christian ↑ makes God and His work in you more real ar dynamic than does my approach, I am content But at least let me insist that you need always to keep the order straight. Put God first, then you; His work, then yours; His initiative, your response; His dynamic, your acceptance of His dynamic.

Let me insist upon it being His life in you. Let me insist upon it all being in no confidence in the flesh. Let Him be first!

Then, if it helps you to emphasize the importance of a disciplined response to His inworking, if you believe that is God's voice to you, please give it heed! It is not possible to stress obedience too much. Just do not try to convince yourself that genuine spiritual obedience to God is humanly possible. Give precedence to the growing relationship of your heart and spirit to God through Christ which alone makes real heart obedience possible.

Real Danger

I hope that I have not given the impression that I advocate total passivity and no personal responsibility on the part of the believer. This is certainly not my wish.

However, this is not my greatest danger, nor is it that of most Christians I know who are seeking to learn to walk humbly with our

d. We are in far greater danger of failing to
rest dependently in Him to be everything we
need to live in a Christianity that really works.

Do's and Don'ts

The demands of the New Testament are so
many and so great that for most of my years I
saw it as a book of law, of things I had to do to
please God. Why, if resting in His life in us is
the secret of spiritual life, should it be so?

First, the carnal Christian isn't ready to
receive rest to replace self-effort. He needs
external direction to keep him from straying
too far from the path of right living.

Second, even external obedience has some
benefits. The temporal blessings such as happi-
er human relationships or healthier bodies are
missed by those who live ungodly lives. Also,
our failure to live up to our standards of obedience may finally force us to depend on the Lord
and His grace.

Finally, since Christ lives in all of His own,
His life all the time working in us, we should
properly understand all the instructions of the
New Testament as given to the new man—the
not I, but Christ in me. They can't be read as
though the independent I were to perform
them. Only the new life that is Christ, His
grace, and His might at work in me is capable.

Rest Versus Activity

Finding a balance between resting in t
Lord and responsible activity is not easy t
achieve or maintain. Perhaps it is not really a
balance that is needed so much as a correct
view of rest and responsibility. Living in the
Lord and His peace is the golden secret of a
Christianity that really works. However, some
of us can easily fall into pretending to live in
the Lord in peace when we are really just being
lazy and unresponsive to God's working in us.

Our minds, hearts, and wills need to be
trained in practical spiritual exercise to respond to the Lord's drawing. Using the faculties God has graciously provided need not be a
work of the flesh, but irresponsibility, laziness,
and carelessness certainly are. A supposed rest
in Christ that more genuinely resembles these
than it does the peace of God is a work of the
flesh. However, to demand of ourselves more
diligent effort than the Spirit has yet produced
in us will also be fleshly.

"Where the Spirit of the LORD is, there is
liberty" (2 Corinthians 3:17). So we must allow
ourselves to be led of the Lord in liberty, free
from demands for supposedly spiritual effort on
one hand or superficial quietness and rest on
the other. Be free of needing to accomplish any
particular thing, to feel peace, or to experience
anything else in order to be content in Christ.

Here is true freedom in the Spirit: to be at ...disposal, to live freely in Him as He lives ...us, to rest content in Him and His peace ...herever we find ourselves and so allow His ...fe to course through us, mightily enabling us to resist the devil, to exercise ourselves energetically unto godliness, and to labor in holy fear so as to bring to completion the salvation He has freely given us. This is the glorious liberty of the children of God.

Instant Experience or Long-term Change

Whatever instant experience you lay claim to must be authenticated by changes in your life that mirror Christ. To lay claim to any experience from God without being emptied of yourself, or without even having any great wish to be, is to play word games and bring disgrace on the name of the Lord. To be pressed by people or doctrine into a premature decision or commitment is to endanger the process by which the Lord is drawing you to Himself in love. To conclude that some experience is all you need to live the Christian life satisfactorily can lead only to frustration and failure, or to living in hypocrisy.

Let any experience with God be only a step forward in your walk with Him. Let it lead to more forward steps as you live looking to Him in increasing dependence for everything.

A Matter of Scale

Trust in the LORD with all your heart,
and lean not on your own understanding,
in all your ways acknowledge Him,
and He shall direct your paths.
—Proverbs 3:5-6

The need of being led and guided by the Spirit of God in more of the details of our lives is a major part of becoming really dependent on the Lord. It is the opposite of being self-dependent. I confess I have much to learn about being sensitive to the Lord's leading in the so-called little things of life.

Often it is difficult to achieve a balance between trying too hard to know God's specific will on whether to go to the bank or the post office first, and on the other hand being insensitive to His special intervention in even such mundane matters. Often we resent the very idea of being this dependent on the Lord. But we will surely find that to be as happy, content, and at peace as we can be, we must.

We may for a time need to be extravagantly sensitive to the possibility of God's specific direction in the little things if we are to learn to hear and recognize His voice clearly. At the same time, being unduly concerned by our failure to be as sensitive as we think we should be might lead to living in bondage.

he secret is to commit your way to the
., release everything to Him, and go on
r way comfortably resting in the peaceful
surance that He is, in fact, in charge. Then
ncreasingly, restfully, allow Him to be.

Afraid of Fear of the Lord

> *My covenant was with him,*
> *one of life and peace,*
> *and I gave them to him*
> *that he might fear Me;*
> *So he feared Me,*
> *and was reverent before My name.*
> —*Malachi 2:5*

> *Fear God.*
> —*1 Peter 2:17*

> *Perfecting holiness in the fear of God.*
> —*2 Corinthians 7:1*

We reject the idea of fearing God as only
belonging to the Old Testament under the law,
when it is very much a New Testament concept
as well. We reject it, thinking it is the opposite
of experiencing and living in God's love. We
reject it because we think the fear of the Lord
would make us unhappy. The truth is that sin,
pretense, and unreality cause unhappiness and
distress. Just as judgment and justice are part

and parcel of God's love, so is godly fear. **T**
reality recognized and accepted gladly mak
us happy and free! *"You shall know the trut.*
and the truth shall make you free" (John 8:32)

To pretend that God is not *"a consuming*
fire" is to play the fool, living in pretense. To
imagine that the fear of God is the opposite of
the love of God is to be misled indeed. To think
the purpose of His fire is to make us miserable
and frightened is folly. The fire of His love
consumes only the destructive and hurtful to
set us free, not to make us unhappy.

To accept the goodness of fearing God is
wisdom indeed. *"The fear of the LORD is the*
beginning of wisdom" (Proverbs 9:10). To fear
God is not, as we tend to think, the opposite of
living contentedly accepted in the beloved. It is
not to make us perpetually uncomfortable in
Him. It is to know that displeasing Him is to
act destructively toward ourselves, others, and
all that is good. It is to know that pleasing Him
is the greatest happiness we can find.

The lack of this fear of God limits our
maturing spiritually. An important part of the
motivation to godliness is missing, leaving
Christianity emasculated, without virility and
spiritual dynamic. Deep inside where our inner
drives and motivations lie buried, we think we
can do as we want without cost to us. In effect,
we think that we can put one over on God, a
god we've put in chains to a misconceived love.

To fear God is simply to recognize and live the reality that God is both loving and just, Savior and Lord, Redeemer and Judge. It is to recall that we will answer to Him someday for the deeds done in the body. It is to know that in order to be love, He must hate sin as that which destroys. Finally He must destroy the destructive force of sin so that love may eternally reign supreme.

We must flee the plague of erratic swings of theology from period to period. Our present-day theology has emasculated God and made Him a softy. This is not at all necessary to maintain His limitless love. The fiercest of beasts are the most tender with their offspring. At the same time, they're capable of training and disciplining them to be strong and mature.

To fear God rightly is to see God as pure and holy, delightful, attractive and precious on the one hand. On the other, it is to accept deliverance from our desire to hide from a hideous God manufactured by the devil's lies.

He is more lovely because He is balanced and complete. If His love incapacitated Him to judge the sin and sinners that could destroy all which is good, He would be incapable of loving us enough to purge the world. He would be incapacitated to return wholeness, health, love, gentleness, kindness, beauty, and joy unlimited to His universe. He wouldn't be God!

CHAPTER 31

Final Thoughts on Christ at Work

Being confident of this very thing,
that He who has begun a good work in you
will complete it until the day of Jesus Christ.
—Philippians 1:6

I find everywhere in Christendom works! Not His work, but ours. Not quiet neediness of Spirit, but our accomplishment. Not rest in His life, but striving in ours, sometimes even under the guise of its being His.

One of the worst works errors is the demand that we change, that we decide for Christ, that we obey God, that we have faith in Him, that we will to please Him, even that we bring ourselves to the place of letting God's life replace ours, His peace and rest replace our striving. We cannot. He can and must at His pace, in His way, in His time. We must rather look to Him in anticipation of His doing it, and wait restfully, peacefully, meekly for Him to do so, rather than try to force it on ourselves.

***

...etheless, in order for Him to do His ...n us, we must respond to our Lord's life-love-call. The chief factor in spiritual ...nation may be that we do not seek Him ...st, and as a result, we do not find Him and ...ith Him the all He offers us. There are too ...many other things first for us, and they are all idols replacing God.

By holding out on the Lord, by preferring our idols to Him, we limit what He can do in, for, and through us. We limit the free flow of His life in us. God help us to have no confidence in the flesh. Then His life will flow in us, as we have no other. How delightful!

***

It is neither our responsibility to originate the desire nor provide the capacity to be conformed to His image. It is our responsibility to let Him unstop the blockages so His life can flow freely in us by exposing ourselves to the cleansing of His Word and His Spirit; letting go, as He enables, of all the blockages of self, rights, possessions, and control; letting Him reveal our need and Himself our all-sufficient supply; and letting Him teach us to come to Him, trust Him, rest content in Him, and depend on Him for all things.

***

The Spirit of God alone can work the work of God in our hearts and lives. He alone can make God real, living, personal, and vital to us.

Only He can work the transformation in hearts and lives. He alone can make it possi... for us to live in intimate fellowship with th... Lord. He, as God, makes the Christianity w... profess really work.

But let's not be confused. Merely having correct doctrine about the work of God and His Spirit is not enough. We need to know the Spirit Himself—real, personal, living, and active. Just knowing about God is of little value if we do not know, trust and rely on Him as He is. Let's release all else, even our supposed knowledge of Him, to receive Him and from Him as He is.

***

We will benefit greatly if, early on in our communion with God, we recognize that our minds, hearts, and attitudes are filled with misperceptions that severely cripple us. Recognizing their presence and longing to have them corrected is a part of the humility without which growth in our relationship with the Lord can't occur.

Meditating on God and His truth impacts our misperceptions of reality, including our misperceptions of God. See Psalm 1:1-2 and Psalm 119. As the Spirit uses the Word to correct our misperceptions, we'll see Him more nearly as He really is with both our minds and our spirits. This in turn will lead us to respond to Him more appropriately.

In turn, these right responses will work to ⁓rect our attitudes and actions not only ⁓ward Him but toward ourselves, others, and ⁓ll things.

***

We want to recognize and live without undue discouragement with the reality of our continuing rebellion, resistance, and resentment toward God and His control of our lives. But we must be sure there isn't the least acceptance or approval of either our sinfulness or our acts of sin. Rather, we must long for more deliverance from them. Looking to the Lord alone as our hope, we can live in quiet confidence in Him to do the transforming work.

***

Our whole Christian walk is based on basic trust in God. We must never find Him less than entirely trustworthy in all circumstances, no matter how hurtful, frightening, desperate, long continued, and impossible they may appear, or how silent God may seem to be.

When there's nothing to do and no place to go, just trust Him. If it seems you can't trust because you're too hurt, too worn out, too scared, too whatever, tell him you feel like you can't trust Him, but there's just nothing else for you to do. Just lay down in His arms, and let Him hold you tight. If you don't feel like it, if you try to trust Him and rest in Him and you can't, just stop and offer Him the little trust you have. Even if it is only mist. offer it to Him, and stop your struggling.

***

I am increasingly conscious of the awfu threat to our entire Christian walk, and espe cially to the transformation of our character into the likeness of our Lord's, posed by our terrible prideful desire to control. Husbands want to control wives, wives to control husbands, both to control children, and children to control parents. We all want to set the other guy straight. No one will accept the obvious fact that others will act the way they will act, and nothing can be done to change it.

Both want to be in charge. Neither wants to back off and let God be in charge. But that is the only way to get along with people and yourself, for that matter. Let God be in charge.

***

Until we reach the place of brokenness before the Lord, our capacity to surrender to Him is limited. Our independent spirit must be broken—our inner willfulness, pride, and self-dependence. Until it is, there will be more of superficiality and pretense than there will be of reality about any claim to living in resignation to His will. Nor is there really a thing we can do about it but ask Him for willingness to give Him permission to do the breaking.

Remember the horse. He is broken to the saddle and the bridle. His independent will is

...en so he may be a contented and useful ...panion and help to his master.

***

To take up your cross is to live in subjection to God rather than to your independent self. It is to live by what He wants, not from the external demand and pressure of the law, but from an inner drawing of love, not with clenched teeth because you have to, but from humble trust in God who asks nothing of you that is not the very best for you.

***

Scripture repeatedly shows that we are to expect to suffer for Christ's sake so long as we live in this world. It shows the benefits received by those who suffer.

A great deal of our problem is that we are not willing to suffer. I have written more than once in my prayer journal, "Struggling with accepting what He has for me of pain today," or "Struggling again. Realized I wasn't content to accept all He sends as good for me."

We are afraid—afraid of pain, afraid of trouble, afraid of losing what we have, afraid of inadequate supply to meet our needs, afraid of what people think of us, afraid of making mistakes and suffering the difficult results. Paul, on the other hand, looked at *"the fellowship of His* [Christ's] *sufferings"* as a vital part of knowing Christ.

312

If the Lord goes with me into the s—
if He tailors it to meet my need to kno—
better, if He will comfort and hold me,
will enable me not so much to feel the suffe—
as to see Him better in it, then can't I put
fears aside in favor of simply trusting a—
worshiping Him, relaxing into His love rathe—
than being terrorized by my pain and fear?

So long as I have other wants than Him,
even if it is just to be comfortable, I will continue to struggle. What I want is what I worship.
May I find myself set free from my fears by
wanting only Him, worshiping only Him. May
I want above all else that He be fully my God.

***

Here on earth, we have no continuing city.
This is not our home. Placing no significant
value on the temporal and physical, only on the
eternal and spiritual, we look forward to our
future home.

We claim to be citizens of that heavenly
city, yet we think little of it. Sermons on it
seem so rare. Our conversations seem almost
deliberately to exclude it. While it may not be
quite true, it sometimes seems that we mourn
almost as those who have no hope.

Let's lift our eyes. Let's look to the Lord.
Let's get excited about seeing Him face to face
and living in His love forevermore.

***

children of Israel wandered in the
...or forty years when they could have
the trek in a few weeks. Why? Because
grumbled and complained at a grumpy
.? Hardly! Rather, in their hearts they were
scontent and unthankful to the God of love
who was seeking for them the best they could
be given. By their discontent and unthankful-
ness, they shut the door on what He would
have given them. As a result all but Caleb and
Joshua died in the desert when they could have
lived in the land of milk and honey. What was
the problem at its heart? They mistrusted God!

Is your tongue thankful? Is your heart
content with what God dishes out to you? If
not, look out!

***

Without faith it is impossible to please Him.
—Hebrews 11:6

This faith is not of our working. It is His
gift. It is trust that rests quietly, dependently
on what He has done and is doing as adequate
for all our needs.

***

The utmost in personal responsibility,
submission, and dependence on God is to have
quiet confidence in Him. I trust Him to work.
I get out of His way and wait contentedly for
Him to tell me when He wants me to do

something, what He wants me to do, and
He wants me to do it.

***

God continues to show us His way mor
perfectly. As we go on, we may see things
differently. I learn it is not important that I
worship God after any particular fashion, as I
once thought it was, only that I respond appropriately to the wonder of who He is. I realize it
is not important that my love for Him be
deeply felt, only that I respond to His love
working in me with a desire to give myself to
Him and to please Him. I discover it is not so
much that I seek Him, but that I respond to
Him as He seeks me out for Himself. I recognize that is not so much that I come to Him,
but that I respond as He comes to me.

At last I may understand that all of my
activity must succumb to His activity and I
become only the recipient and the channel. As
much as there is to learn, if I will but abide in
Him, comfortable with His doing, increasingly
willing to respond with all His enabling to all
He does, everything else will follow.

***

Let's build our lives on our Lord and on
the truth that He is in us performing all that is
necessary for our eternal benefit. We are in
Him where we can live confidently, contentedly
at home, assured He is always doing His all-
sufficient work on our behalf. We can rest

ent in the divine reality that He is in us,
king His divine transformation.

He is working in us even the capacity to
est and trust in Him, to remain or abide in
Him, to contentedly accept His working, even
His causing us to will and to do of His good
pleasure. True, often we are not very aware
that it is occurring. Still, we can know it is
because He says so. What release! What joy!
What life!

Addendum

The Christianity that really works
is Christ Himself.
Christ in us is all we need.
We are complete in Him.

It is God's purpose
to make us happy and satisfied in Him
through all eternity.
He wants to give us the beginning
of this eternal joy now
in spite of the pain and distress
we all experience
in a sinning, hurting, and hurtful world.

It is the devil's greatest lie
that convinces us to see loving God
and doing what pleases Him as an obligation.
In reality it is the most wonderful privilege
granted the human race,
and the ultimate secret of human happiness.

The God of all the universe has given Himself
to us in love.
Is it possible we would refuse to seek Him
and with Him all He offers?

s it possible that we would prefer
ntinue in our long-established patterns
of rebellion and self-destruction?

Oh, may it not be so for you or me.

We who are His by faith in Christ are in Him
Who is our life and our all,
accepted in the beloved,
living in His righteousness, under His blood.
He who is our life and our all is in us
providing us, with Himself, all we need.

Our part is to worship and adore Him,
and watch Him teach us
to rest content in Him in childlike trust,
and so be changed into His likeness
from glory to glory for His eternal praise.
In order to rest at home in Him,
we must let go, as nearly as He enables,
of everything but Him, resigning ourselves
and everything that touches us
into His control.

The problem is that
the rebellious human heart doesn't want
to hear, understand, or accept
this simple necessity.
We don't want to
die to our independent selves,
so we can't live fully to Him.

But as He teaches us
to rest contentedly at home in Him
in trusting love,
His all-sufficient life will flow freely in us
and overflow to other hurting hearts.
His life will increasingly replace
the life of the independent self.
And with His gifts
of trust, and love, and rest, and peace,
He will gentle us, gradually developing in us
a meek and sensitive spirit,
resigned to Him and His plans,
eager to please Him and serve others.

Increasingly emptied
of our independent selves,
dead to our supposed capabilities,
we are being filled with Him,
becoming dependent on His abilities.

Still, we mustn't be surprised
if we find ourselves,
for a remarkably long period of time,
even in a sincere pursuit of the Lord,
continuing unwittingly down the wide road
of self-effort and works-righteousness.
Nor must we be surprised
at the pain and suffering
God graciously allows in our lives.

only by such means may He bring us
ultimately to the end of ourselves,
where we actually know
that without Him we can do nothing.
Only so may we come to the beginning
of His being our all.

The wonder is
that the great God of all the universe
is personally overseeing everything
that touches our lives
to make it all work together
for our eternal benefit.
The One who with a word
spoke uncounted millions of heavenly bodies
into existence
cares for our every need!

What else would it take to make us
happy and contented
in the midst of the pain of a sinning world?
What else would it take to make us
excited about learning to live in Him
and receive, in Him, all He so freely offers?
What else would it take to make us
want to please Him,
and so enjoy Him the more fully,
and, with Him,
all the delights He so freely offers,
now and through all of a perfect eternity?
Praise His glorious name.